THE NEW COVENANT CHURCH -*EKKLESIA*- OF CHRIST

John G. Reisinger

Books by
John G. Reisinger

Abraham's Four Seeds

The Believer's Sabbath

But I Say Unto You

Chosen in Eternity

Christ, Lord and Lawgiver Over the Church

Continuity and Discontinuity

Grace

The Grace of Our Sovereign God

In Defense of Jesus, the New Lawgiver

John Bunyan on the Sabbath

Limited Atonement

The New Birth

New Covenant Theology and Prophecy

Our Sovereign God

Perseverance of the Saints

Studies in Galatians

Studies in Ecclesiastes

Tablets of Stone

The Sovereignty of God and Prayer

The Sovereignty of God in Providence

Total Depravity

What is the Christian Faith?

When Should a Christian Leave a Church?

THE NEW COVENANT CHURCH
-*EKKLESIA*-
OF CHRIST

John G. Reisinger

5317 Wye Creek Drive, Frederick, MD 21703-6938
301-473-8781 | info@newcovenantmedia.com
www.NewCovenantMedia.com

THE NEW COVENANT CHURCH
-EKKLESIA-
OF CHRIST

Copyright 2014 © by
Sovereign Grace New Covenant Ministries

Cover design by: Laura D. Bonser

Published by: New Covenant Media
                     5317 Wye Creek Drive
                     Frederick, MD 21703-5938

Orders: www.newcovenantmedia.com

Printed in the United States of America.

ISBN 13: 978-1-928965-59-6

Dedication

This book is dedicated to the memory of a godly man and faithful pastor. Don McKinney paid a high price for his belief in sovereign grace. He was never more like his patron saint, Martin Luther, than when he refused to deny or soft pedal the doctrine of election knowing he could lose everything. He said, "I would rather sell bananas for a nickel each than deny that I owe all my salvation to the sovereign election of God." I owe him much. He was my friend and my mentor.

Table of Contents

Chapter One
The Called Out Ones

Since the English word *church* is totally unrelated to the Greek word *ekklesia,* the word the Holy Spirit chose to use in the Scriptures, I will use *ekklesia* instead of *church* until we arrive at a definition.

One of the first difficulties in defining the word *ekklesia* is determining whether there are two different definitions for the word when it is applied to Christians. All agree the word is used for both a secular and a spiritual group. What about when the *ekklesia* is talking about the people of God? Does the New Testament Scripture use the word *ekklesia* two distinctly different ways or only one way? Almost all theologians since the time of the Reformation have spoken of the 'universal' (or invisible) and the 'local' (or visible) *ekklesia* and given different definitions for both concepts. Different groups have emphasized one or the other of these two ideas.

The Plymouth Brethren magnify the universal/invisible concept. They insist the *ekklesia* is an 'organism' and not an 'organization.' They have no church membership (on paper), and no 'ordained clergymen.' Roman Catholicism and Landmark Baptists emphasize the local/visible concept of *ekklesia.* In their view the *ekklesia* is a visible physical organization, instead of an invisible organism, instituted by Christ and left in control of duly authorized leaders here on earth. Landmark Baptists call the universal *ekklesia* concept the 'doctrine of the great spiritual whore,' and Rome insists that one of the four marks of 'the one true church' is that the true church is 'visible.' Here are two quotes setting forth the Landmark position:

> ... the New Testament usage of the term *[ekklesia]* ... denotes an assembly or a gathered group, a congregation. ...[1]

> ... The words "church" and "assembly" are therefore synonymous. It is, therefore, essential for a "church" to "church" before it can be a "church"! That is, an "assembly" must "assemble" before it can be an "assembly." A "church" which has never assembled or met together in an organized fashion and for a specific purpose, never having been functional, would certainly not be a "church" in the scriptural sense![2]

As you can see, such a definition eliminates any possibility of a so-called 'universal/invisible' *ekklesia*. The *ekklesia* must be visibly assembled before it is an *ekklesia*. Any idea of the redeemed people of God bowing their hearts in worship all over the world being construed as the *ekklesia* is ridiculous to these people. There must be a visible gathering of individuals bound together under some form of constitution with leadership ordained by God and given authority to rule the *ekklesia*. This same group of individuals is not considered the *ekklesia* when they finish assembling and go their separate ways. It is only when they are 'assembled' that they are considered the *ekklesia*.

Mr. Downing uses the typical Landmark Baptist caricature of the 'universal church' to establish his position.

---

[1] W.R. Downing, *The New Testament Church* (Morgan Hill, CA, PIRS Publications, 2006) 10.

[2] Ibid., 16, 17.

A "Universal, Invisible Church" could have:
- No address or location, yet every church in the New Testament was located at a particular place…
- No pastor, elders or spiritual leadership that was functional or operational.
- No deacons or property …
- No treasurer …
- No prayer meetings …
- No missionaries… [3]

It may seem strange that the Romanists and the Landmark Baptists are both so adamant against any idea of a 'universal' church. However, when we see that their respective concepts of authority are almost identical, it becomes very clear why they are kinfolk. Every group that emphasizes 'God ordained authority' for either their particular church practices or the authority of their 'duly authorized leadership' will always emphasize the so-called 'local/visible' church as the true *ekklesia* of Christ. Baptists who do this can be just as tyrannical as Roman Catholics. We will say more about this later. For now, I intend to argue that there is only one definition of the word *ekklesia* in the New Testament Scriptures even though there are two applications of the one definition.

The first question we must ask is, "What is the best way to translate the Greek word *ekklesia?*" Some people go into the various words used to define the meaning of 'church' in many different languages, such as Scottish *kirk*. This may explain history but it does not help us at all to grasp Scripture. The Plymouth Brethren use the word *assembly* and some other groups use *congregation*, but nearly

---

[3] Ibid., 18.

everyone uses the word _church_ which means nothing. I personally, until recently, would have said that 'assembly' was probably the best way to translate _ekklesia._ I would no longer do that. I would now translate it so that it clearly expresses exactly what everyone agrees is the actual meaning of the word. I would translate _ekklesia_ as the 'called out ones' since that is precisely what the word means. This is not only the true and accurate translation of the word _ekklesia,_ it also demonstrates the first major truth, namely, that the _ekklesia_ of Christ is _they,_ meaning _people,_ and not _it,_ meaning an _organization._ If you cannot speak of the _ekklesia_ as 'they' but constantly think and speak in terms of 'it' you have not totally come out of Romanism!

Usually, the first thing we do in trying to understand a specific doctrine in Scripture is translate the actual meaning of the word itself as clearly as possible into our language. We do that with words like _justification, sanctification, and regeneration._ However, when we come to the word _ekklesia_ we use the word _church_ instead of actually translating the word _ekklesia_ into its English equivalent. _Ekklesia_ literally means the 'called out ones' and should be so translated. In failing to do that we ignore the first basic step that we otherwise always follow when trying to understand any specific doctrine. We always try, whether it is a Greek or a Hebrew word, to translate the word as closely as possible to an English word, or words. We try to stick as closely as we can to the original Greek or Hebrew. If we did that in the case of _ekklesia_ we would say without hesitation, "the word _ekklesia_ means 'called out (ones)'."

The reluctance to translate _ekklesia_ as 'called out ones' may be an honest mistake, but it may also be that we do not want to destroy the basic concepts that we have, and constantly use the *"ekklesia* of Christ."* For instance, if ekklesia means 'they,' or people, and not 'it,' meaning an organization, it has far-reaching implications. If ekklesia is correctly translated 'called out ones' there will never, among other things, ever be another unregenerate child sprinkled with water in 'baptism' because it is believed that he* is a part of the 'called out ones' (the *ekklesia*) by physical birth. That would be seen as an open contradiction, and so it would be. Many men who baptize babies will agree with what I just said. They freely admit their whole view of infant baptism rests solely on their view of the nature of the *ekklesia*. Here is one example from respected scholar Charles Hodge.

> Infant Baptism. The difficulty on the subject of infant baptism is that baptism from its very nature involves a profession of faith. It is the way in which Christ is to be confessed before men. But infants are incapable of making such a confession; therefore they are not the proper subjects of baptism. To state the difficulty in another form: The sacraments belong to the members of the Church, i.e., the company of believers. Since infants cannot exercise faith, they are not members of the Church and consequently ought not to be baptized.
>
> In order to justify the baptism of infants, we must attain and authenticate such an idea of the Church as to include the children of believing parents …[4]

And guess what, by applying logic to his Covenant Theology, Hodge manages to 'deduce' a view of the church

---

[4] Charles Hodge, *Systematic Theology, Abridged Edition* (Phillipsburg, NJ, P&R Publishing, 1992) 484.

that will **justify** baptizing babies. The real difference between a Baptist and a Presbyterian is not primarily over infant baptism *per se* but over the nature of the *ekklesia*. This is why the *paedobaptist* puts such an emphasis on baptizing babies. He is willing to distort Scripture to find what is not there just to have an excuse to include the baby in the *ekklesia*, even while denying that every 'covenant' child is one of the elect or one of the 'called out ones.' He admits there are both Jacobs and Esaus among the 'covenant' children. Our difference is over defining the *ekklesia*. If we would just use the correct translation, the 'called out ones,' there would be no problem unless you would also believe that every 'covenant' child, without exception, is one of the elect by virtue of being born into a Christian home. If the *ekklesia*, the 'called out ones,' are the only biblical objects of baptism, then everything hinges on the nature of the *ekklesia*.

Infant baptism is the grandmother of many errors. It has disastrous results over a period of time. Its real error is in corrupting the biblical nature of the *ekklesia* of Christ. The paedobaptist admits that it is not God's will for the *ekklesia*, in his definition, to include only believers. He is forced to this absurdity in order to get unregenerate babies into the *ekklesia* of Christ. Let me again quote Charles Hodge. Notice his use of the phrase 'visible church.' As we shall see later, when men like Hodge use the 'visible/invisible' concept of the *ekklesia* they are miles away from what a Baptist means when he may use those same terms.

> *(2) The Visible Church does not consist exclusively of the Regenerate.* There are several indications that it is not the

purpose of God that the visible Church on earth should consist
exclusively of true believers: ...[5]

Hodge, and other Presbyterians, insists that if a Baptist
church has one unsaved member then the whole 'regenerate
membership' concept is destroyed. We respond that an
individual's membership based on a *false* profession of faith
and a membership based on a *non-profession* of faith are two
different things. Accepting a hypocrite (only because we
cannot see his heart) who has made a false confession of
faith is a totally different matter than knowingly saying
unbelievers are truly members of the *ekklesia*. As I said, the
Baptist concept of a 'visible/invisible' *ekklesia* is radically
different than a paedobaptist's view. The *ekklesia* as
'believers only' and the church as 'believers and *their
children*' are two totally different concepts that have far-
reaching consequences. We will say more about this later.

Nearly all of the problems now being discussed in our
chat rooms would be answered differently if everyone
involved had a clear view of the true meaning of the '*ekklesia*
of Christ.' Issues like who should take communion, who
should be baptized, when and how discipline should take
place, the authority of eldership, etc., would all be looked at
differently.

Let's look at the biblical meaning of *ekklesia*. All agree that
the Greek word *ekklesia* is really a compound of two Greek
words. The first word is *ek*, and means 'out,' and the second
is *kaleo* (kal-eh'-o) and means 'to call.'

All agree that the word *kaleo* means to 'to call' or 'called
ones,' and the word *ekklesia* literally means the same thing

---

[5] Ibid., 485.

except with the addition of the word *ek*. This means we merely add the word 'out' and it becomes 'the called out ones.' As I said, everyone agrees this is the literal meaning of the word *kaleo* and the word *ekklesia*. All Reformed and Calvinistic people agree that this calling, when used to describe a Christian, is talking about regeneration or effectual calling. It has nothing to do with 'calling an individual to join a local congregation.' In fact, biblical calling is totally spiritual and has nothing to do with the physical. We need only note a few verses where the word is used to clearly understand its meaning. These verses show that the 'kaleoed' and the 'Christians' are the same people.

Galatians 1:6 *"I marvel that ye are so soon removed from him that **called** you into the grace of Christ unto another gospel ..."*

Does joining a local congregation have anything at all to do with being called *(kaleoed)* into the 'grace of Christ'?

Galatians 1:15 *"But when it pleased God, who separated me from my mother's womb, and **called** me by his grace..."*

Did this calling have anything to do with Paul joining a local congregation or in any way coming under the authority of a local congregation?

A shorter form, *klesis (klay'-sis)*, of the same word, is often used. Here are a few instances.

Romans 11:29 *"For the gifts and **calling** of God are without repentance."*

What does that text have to do with membership in a local congregation? What do any of the following texts have to do with anything other than spiritual effectual calling?

Ephesians 4:4 *"There is one body, and one Spirit, even as ye are called in one hope of your **calling**..."*

Philippians 3:14 *"I press toward the mark for the prize of the high **calling** of God in Christ Jesus."*

Hebrews 3:1 *"Wherefore, holy brethren, partakers of the heavenly **calling**..."*

Did any local congregation, or any, or all, of the other apostles, or anyone else have anything to do with God calling Paul in the following verse? Remember this is the same word used in *ekklesia.* **Romans 1:1** "Paul, a servant of Jesus Christ, **called** to be an apostle..."

What does the *calling* in the following verses have to do with the concept of a local congregation? These verses are talking about regeneration, about being joined to Christ. The word *ekklesia* is talking about being 'called out' of death and being brought into Christ. The word has nothing to do with either defining or joining a local congregation.

Romans 1:6 *"Among whom are ye also **the called** of Jesus Christ..."* Romans 1:7 *"To all that be in Rome, beloved of God, **called to be saints...**"* Romans 8:28 *"And we know that all things work together for good to them that love God, to them who are **the called** according to his purpose."*

Is Romans 8:28 assuring us that all is well because we are a member of a local congregation, or because we are part of the *ekklesia* of Christ? I am sure you know the answer. I am also sure you realize that the two things just mentioned, membership in a local congregation and being a part of the 'called ones' *(ekklesia)* of Christ, are two totally different things. It is in understanding why these two things are so radically different that opens up the biblical doctrine of the *ekklesia.*

I think it is easy to see that the words the 'called ones' are nothing less than another name for a Christian. A child of

God is called, a 'believer,' a 'sheep,' an 'elect one,' a 'brother,' a 'saved one,' etc., and the same person is often labeled or addressed as a *called one*.' The above texts are clear. The *ekklesia* are Christians. All Christians are in the *ekklesia* and no one but chosen sheep are a part of the *ekklesia*. All of the *ekklesia* have been 'called out' to Christ himself. It is the experience of being *kaleoed* out of the world that makes them Christians. They did not join the *ekklesia* — they were joined to the *ekklesia* by the Holy Spirit.

Let's take that descriptive name, 'called out ones', and ask these obvious questions:

(1) Who is included in this group described by the Holy Spirit as the *ekklesia,* or 'called out ones'?

(2) Who is the Person who is calling, or has called, the *ekklesia?*

(3) To where or to what have the *ekklesia* been called?

(4) From where, or what, have the *ekklesia* been called out from?

(5) Why have these particular ones been 'called out' to the exclusion of others?

(6) What is the exact nature of this calling?

I think all Calvinistic and Reformed people will answer (1) this way: The 'called out ones' are the people of God. They are the 'sheep who hear my voice' and gladly respond. They are the saved, the justified, and the born again who have been baptized into the living body of Christ. Simply put, the 'called out ones' is a synonym for the word 'Christian.' The *ekklesia* is another name for saved people — all saved people, but only saved people. It is impossible to have a lost person in the *ekklesia,* or among the 'called out ones,' and it is just as impossible to have a saved person who is not a member of the *ekklesia*. Both of these things would be a contradiction in terms.

Likewise, there will be no disagreement among sovereign grace people concerning, (2) who the Person is who is doing the calling. We need only one glance at the texts above to see it is God himself who is the 'Caller' in every case. The calling is directly due to both God's purpose in unconditional election and his sovereign power in regeneration. It has nothing to do with man's will or an organization.

As to where they have been called, (3) we can say that ultimately they have been called to heaven itself. We can also say they are 'called to holiness,' 'called to peace,' 'called to life,' and many other things. For our purposes, we insist that the 'called out ones' are called into membership in the *ekklesia* of Christ. Each 'called one,' or each member of the *ekklesia*, has been effectually called out of sin and death into a living fellowship with Christ himself.

(4) All of the 'called out ones' were once dead in sin. It was 'the call' that brought them out of death and brought them into life. Their calling is spoken of as a resurrection from the dead as well as regeneration.

(5) The 'called out ones' are the same as the elect. All of the elect are 'called' and all 'the called' are the elect. All of the sheep, the elect ones, will always 'hear' the voice of their Shepherd calling them and will gladly come. All of the 'called out ones' become part of the *ekklesia* simply because they, and they alone, are the objects of this special 'calling,' and they are the special objects because they have been chosen to be sheep. *All* the chosen are 'called' but *only* the

chosen are 'called.' That is the same as saying, "All the elect are in the *ekklesia*, but only the elect are in the *ekklesia*." There is not a single exception to this fact, and we must again emphasize that being a 'called out one' has nothing to do with birth, baptism, or joining something.

(6) This calling is nothing less than effectual calling. The 'calling' extended to the elect sheep is actually regeneration. It is being born again and in no sense whatever is it 'joining something.' It is 100% spiritual and it is 100% the work of God, and in every case it is successful. The *ekklesia*, or 'called out ones,' will have no missing members. All *without exception* who are chosen to be in the *ekklesia* will be effectually called by grace and power and will become a living part of the *ekklesia*. Again, this fact has nothing to do with any or all visible congregations. Someone has said, "**The** church will be found in the churches, but the churches are not **the** church."

I should not have to make this application, but I do so for clarity. The reality, or actual spiritual entity, that is created by this calling of the *ekklesia* is the spiritual body of Christ and it cannot possibly have anything to do with a physical organization. We are talking about a spiritual calling. If the *kaleo*, or **calling,** that creates the *ekklesia* of Christ is nothing less than regeneration, then the thing created by that spiritual calling, namely, the true *ekklesia*, must of necessity be a God-produced *spiritual creation*. It has to be first of all a living spiritual entity. The words 'called out ones' cannot possibly have anything at all to do with the physical organization or assembling of that which we today call a 'church.' The spiritual experience of effectual calling (*kaleo*) creates, in and of itself, the *ekklesia* of Christ, and since that effectual calling (*kaleo*) is totally spiritual it follows that the thing created by that calling, the *ekklesia*, must also be spiritual and not physical.

What we will see as we proceed is that the whole 'visible/invisible' or 'local/universal' concepts expressed by those terms are simply not biblical ideas. They do express an element of truth but they are also loaded with error. At the most we may say, "The Word of God recognizes that the word *ekklesia* basically means 'Christians.' Sometimes an apostle will speak of all Christians, the elect, or all of the 'called out ones' of Christ, and other times he may speak of all the Christians, or all the 'called out ones' meeting in a given town or even in a house. However, in both cases the basic meaning of the word *ekklesia* remains the same. It means the 'called out (ones),' or Christians, in both cases." The difference is not a 'local/visible' versus a 'universal/invisible' concept where one is an organism and the other is an organization. The only difference is how many of the 'called out ones' you are talking about. In both cases the word means 'all of the Christians'–either all for whom Christ died or all those in a given described area.

Men can, and do, create organizations and call them churches or fellowships, but only God the Holy Ghost can create the *ekklesia* of Christ. The *ekklesia* that God creates is the body of Christ. Every person in that *ekklesia* is 'in Christ.' When man creates a physical organization and calls it a 'church' it will be a mixed bag. As long as we argue about 'visible/invisible' or 'local/universal' as a means of distinguishing between a 'spiritual' (universal) *ekklesia* and a 'physical' (local) *ekklesia*, we are missing the real problem. The real question is this: Does the New Testament Scripture conceive of the _ekklesia_, the 'called out ones,' as a spiritual organism created by the Holy Spirit or a physical organization created by men of like mind? Is the body of Christ (which is never spoken of in the plural) ever conceived of as anything less than all of the 'called out ones,' or the '_ekklesia_ of Christ'?

Let me mention another obvious implication. If any individual person evidences the spiritual marks of being one of Christ's sheep, or a 'called out one' can they be denied total acceptance in a group claiming to be a sheepfold of Christ? Dare we say, "I know that Christ, the great Shepherd, has put his mark of grace on you and sealed you with his Spirit. He has unconditionally accepted you as one of his 'called out ones,' however, before we will accept you into this sheepfold, or before we allow you to eat with us at his table, we must put our mark on you also."

Nothing I have said rules out the need for an organized local congregation of like-minded Christians with a constitution, church officers, church discipline, and a lot of other things. I believe every child of God should be a part of a congregation of Christians and submit to the love and oversight of their brothers and sisters in Christ. However, that does not do away with either my personal responsibility to Christ or to all of my 'called out' brothers and sisters in other congregations. What it does mean is that in everything connected with our idea of _ekklesia_, we have to make sure we do not believe and practice a lot of things that grow out of a totally wrong view of the _ekklesia_, or the 'called out ones.'

In the next chapter we will talk about the so-called 'visible/invisible' or 'local/universal' concepts and where they came from. Their first known use by the Reformers in their fight with Rome is very instructive.

Chapter Two
Authority

In chapter one we established that the Greek word *ekklesia* is best translated the 'called out ones.' All agree that this is the basic meaning of the word. The moment we begin to think and talk about the *'ekklesia* of Christ' as the 'called out ones,' we have established the first essential truth about the subject, namely, that the *ekklesia* of Christ means *people*, and not an *it*, meaning an *organization*. The *ekklesia* is some*body* not some*thing*. If you cannot speak of the *ekklesia* as 'they' but instead you constantly think and speak in terms of 'it,' then you have not totally come out of Romanism! The *ekklesia* of Christ is people, the 'called out ones,' and not an organization.

The question is not, "Is there both a universal/invisible and a local/visible church in the New Testament Scriptures?" We have already seen that *ekklesia* has only one definition even though it has two different applications. Actually, the question is not "which of the two concepts of *ekklesia* is the one spoken of the most often in the New Testament Scriptures (NTS)?" It is obvious that there is an *ekklesia* for which Christ died that includes all believers in all ages. It is just as obvious all of the living believers in a given place are called the *ekklesia* of that particular place. The *ekklesia* that includes all of the 'called out ones' is identical to Christ's body which includes every believer as a living part; it is the true temple that includes every believer as a living stone. It is the true nation of God where every citizen is born of God. We could go on and on. This is beyond question the aspect that the NTS emphasize. Theologians have labeled this *ekklesia* the 'universal/invisible' *ekklesia*. Sometimes they use the word *organism* to describe this *ekklesia*. Webster defines *organism* this way:

Organism *noun*

1. An individual form of life, such as a plant, an animal, a bacterium, a protist, or a fungus; a body made up of organs, organelles, or other parts that work together to carry on the various processes of life.

2. A system regarded as analogous in its structure or functions to a living body: *the social organism.*

As J.C. Ryle said so clearly, "This is the true church to which a man must belong, if he would be saved."[6] This *ekklesia* is synonymous with the mystical but real body of Christ.

The Landmark Baptists, along with Rome, insist there is no such thing as a universal/invisible *ekklesia*. They are convinced the only *ekklesia* in the NTS is the local/visible *ekklesia*. If we ask the question another way, the Landmark Baptist and the Romanist miss the boat. Instead of asking whether the visible or invisible *ekklesia* is the most used concept in the NTS, let's ask this question: "Do the NTS emphasize union with Christ via the indwelling Holy Spirit, which all agree is true of all Christians, or do they emphasize membership in a local congregation of professing Christians?" That is bottom line in the discussion. The moment you try to make the 'local/visible' *ekklesia* to be an institution, or physical organization, which is supposed to

---

[6] http://www.utlm.org/onlineresources/truechurch_jcryle.htm (accessed 12-20-2013).

be Christ's vicar on earth, as opposed to the *ekklesia* being an invisible/universal spiritual organism, you are half way back to Rome.

My contention is that the NTS do not give us two different definitions of the *ekklesia* of Christ. There is not a *spiritual ekklesia* where all who are in it are saved, and a *physical ekklesia* made up of both saved and lost. The moment we allow these two different *kinds* of *ekklesias*, we have denied and changed the basic meaning of *ekklesia* as being the 'called out ones.' The difference between the so-called 'universal' *ekklesia* and 'local' *ekklesia* is not that one is a spiritual *organism* made up of regenerate people and the other is a physical *organization* with both saved and lost in it. There is only one *ekklesia*, and the different uses of the word are only referring to how many of the 'called out ones' you are talking about. In one instance you are talking about all the called out ones, or the *ekklesia* for whom Christ died, and in the other instance you are talking about all those living in Corinth, or wherever, for whom Christ died. The Bible does not talk about the difference between an organization and an organism. The so-called visible *ekklesia* does not take on a life of its own independent of a living relationship with her Lord. The *ekklesia* of Christ does not have an ounce of authority on her own. She speaks for Christ only when she speaks his words. She represents Christ only when she repeats what her Lord has spoken. She cannot say, "Christ has made me his vicar on earth therefore you must obey me without question."

I repeat, the *ekklesia* emphasized in the NTS is not an institution, or organization that you join, but it is a spiritual body into which the Holy Spirit has baptized you.

Everything is determined by the phrases "Christ in you" and "you in Christ." It is this truth that the NTS emphasize.

Should Christians today join a group of Christians and live under the love and discipline of that group as it has defined itself and its beliefs in its constitution? Absolutely! But not because that is the way the early church did it. Where is there a single instance in the NTS of any individual being examined and then joining a 'local church'? Should a group of believers write out their beliefs and rules of conduct and require everyone who wants to join their church to promise to live under those rules? Absolutely! But again, not because that is the way the early church did it. Where do the NTS say that each group of believers wrote a constitution? In the nextchapter, I will attempt to demonstrate why there is such confusion about church polity in our day. We must deal with problems for which we have no clear answers. We struggle with situations that not only did not exist in the apostolic age but also could not have been anticipated in that age.

Some people refuse to be a vital part of a congregation of Christians. They feel they are 'giving up their liberty' when they officially join a group of Christians and submit to their love and discipline. What liberty do they give up? Do they have the liberty to divorce themselves from 'the people of Christ' in their locality and not meet and worship with them? I don't think so. I am spiritually joined to all those who are also joined to Christ our common Lord. Every member of his body is my brother or sister. Do the NTS tell me to do certain things that can only be done by my being a member of a gathered group of his sheep? Yes. Do I have the liberty to be a spiritual lone wolf responsible to no other human beings? Where do the NTS give me the liberty to think and act as if I owe nothing to the *ekklesia* of Christ in my area? What do the many 'one another' passages mean unless I am associated with other sheep?

Should a group of Christ's sheep, if they grow in numbers, call a man to act as their pastor? I would say, in most cases, "Yes," even though we do not have any examples in the NTS of any *ekklesia* either calling or ordaining a pastor. I remember the first Baptist ordination service that I attended. The chairman kept waving the Bible and saying, "We Baptists go by the Book." However, the man never once *opened* the Book to justify a single thing that we did. Should believers organize into a 'visible' group, write a constitution, vote to receive people into their fellowship who show evidence of conversion, and vote to dismiss members who live in deliberate disobedience to the beliefs of the group? I would say 'yes' to all of these things. However, I must add, I do not have a text of Scripture to prove any of those things and *the fact I do not have a text does not bother me at all.*

I can hear the institutionalist cocking his guns. You see, his whole position is built on believing that the NTS give us a clear outline of how to organize a true *ekklesia*, how it should be operated, what kind of government it should follow, who should be in charge, and how it should worship. In this person's mind it is inconceivable that there is no clear form of church government in the NTS. I believe there are clear principles but few absolutes. One thing I am sure about—there is no role model institutional *ekklesia* in the NTS. Such a statement is viewed as "doubting the sufficiency of the Word of God." I call this the 'true church syndrome.' It is a giant myth. There simply is no one clear role model institutional church in the NTS. A lot of the things that every group of believers does "in their church" is based on pure pragmatism _and there is nothing at all wrong with that as long as none of it contradicts Scripture._

We make a great mistake when we do not use the material we have in the NTS when trying to establish a system of worship and procedure for a group of people wishing to be a real part of each other's lives. However, we make just as big a mistake when we try to make the NTS say things it simply does not say. Independents and inter-denominationalists have a tendency to neglect clear Scripture, and the institutionalist has a tendency to make the NTS say far more than they do. Both groups emphasize a different aspect of the _ekklesia_ of Christ, and consequently, one tends toward legalism and the other toward antinomianism.

The visible/invisible and local/universal concepts of _ekklesia_ originated when the Reformers argued with Roman Catholics over the charge that Protestants could not possibly be a true church with a valid ministry since they had no authority. Rome claimed that she alone was the only "one, holy, apostolic, and catholic [meaning universal]" church." The Reformers responded by saying they were also part of "one, holy, apostolic, and catholic" church but it was 'invisible.' All of its parts were joined to Christ himself by a living faith and the gift of the Spirit. Rome rejected any idea of an 'invisible' church and insisted the only church in the Scripture is the visible church built on Saint Peter, the first pope.

It is easy to see both how and why the argument was raised and why there could be no answer that satisfied both sides. Rome wanted the church to be a physical organization over which the pope had absolute control. He viewed himself as the vicar of Christ. The reasoning was quite simple: (1) Christ established, or founded, one institution, or church. This was not an invisible organism; this was a visible organization. (2) Christ gave that one organization the total authority to represent him on this earth. (3) That authority is passed down through the ages from pope to pope. (4) Because she is the one true church [meaning organization] on this earth, she alone can dispense the grace of God, meaning the sacraments, through the holy men that she ordains and gives priestly authority. (5) There can be no salvation apart from being in this one true visible church.

I am sure we see the tremendous difference between the Reformers and the Roman Catholics on their view of the *ekklesia* of Christ. However, the Reformers were not consistent. When arguing with Rome, they insisted that personal union with a risen and invisible Christ was the only essential thing. The *ekklesia*, in their argument, was first of all a spiritual organism. They used this approach to establish their claim to be part of "one holy, apostolic, catholic church." When they argued with the Anabaptist they insisted on a visible *ekklesia* with authority over all those within its geographical territory. They wanted two different kinds of *ekklesia*. Rome saw the *ekklesia* of Christ as purely a visible organization, or institution, that was the vicar of the absent Christ. We can also see why statements like "Christ *instituted* a church" must ultimately lead straight to Rome. If we compare Webster's definition of the word _institution_ with the word _organism_, it will help us to see the different views. It will clarify why I keep insisting that the _ekklesia_ is people and not an "it."

Institution _noun_

1. The act of instituting.

2. a. A custom, practice, relationship, or behavioral pattern of importance in the life of a community or society: _the institutions of marriage and the family_. b. _Informal_. One long associated with a specified place, position, or function.

3. _Abbr_. inst., Inst. a. An established organization or foundation, especially one dedicated to education, public service, or culture. b. The building or buildings housing such an organization.

Men can, and do, create institutions, or organizations, and call them churches or fellowships, but only God the Holy Ghost can create the _ekklesia_ of Christ. The _ekklesia_ that God alone can create is the body of Christ, the house of God, the temple of the Holy Spirit. Every person in that _ekklesia_ is 'in Christ,' baptized into his body, a part of his house, a living stone in his temple. When man creates a physical organization and calls it a 'church' it will always be a mixed bag. As long as we argue about 'visible/invisible' or 'local/universal' as a means of distinguishing between a 'spiritual' (universal) _ekklesia_ and a 'physical' (local) _ekklesia_, we are missing the real problem. The real question is this: Do the New Testament Scriptures speak of the _ekklesia_, the 'called out ones,' as a spiritual organism created by the Holy Spirit in regeneration or a physical organization created by men of like mind? Is the body of Christ (which is never spoken of in the NTS as plural) ever conceived of as anything less than all of the 'called out ones,' or the *ekklesia of Christ*?

As noted above, the struggle to define the *ekklesia* was at the heart of the Reformer's struggle with both the Roman Catholics on one hand and the Anabaptists on the other hand. The bottom line in both cases was the definition of the *ekklesia* of Christ as it related to authority.

In the case of the Reformers versus the Anabaptists the issue was church and state. Leonard Verduin has stated the case clearly:

> The Stepchildren [Anabaptists] believed that the Church of Christ is by definition an element in society, not society as such. Their opponents, the Reformers as well as the Catholics,[7] were unwilling to go along with this; they continued to look upon the Church as coextensive with society.
>
> It has been said of late that Luther was faced with a dilemma, the dilemma of wanting both a confessional Church based on personal faith and a regional Church including all in a given locality. It was this dilemma that gave rise to the Second Front [Anabaptists deserting Luther].
>
> This dilemma was a cruel one. He who thinks of the Church as a community of experiential believers is bound to oppose him who thinks of it as a fellowship embracing all in a given territory; he who operates with the concept of the Church as a society embracing all in a given geographic area must of necessity look askance at him who restricts the Church to the believing ones. The two views cannot be combined; one

---

[7] Many Christians today have forgotten that the Reformers hated and persecuted the Anabaptists just as cruelly as did the Roman Catholics and did so for exactly the same reason. What is even worse is the fact that the Reformers used the same Scripture texts and reasoning in carrying out their reign of terror that the Catholics used.

cancels out the other. In the one view the Church is _Corpus Christi,_ the body of Christ, which consists of believing folk and of them solely; in the other view the Church is _Corpus Christianum,_ the body of a "christened" society. As we shall see, attempts have been made to combine these two, but without success.

Upon the horns of this dilemma Luther was impaled. And not only Luther—all the rest of the Reformers were torn between the same two alternatives. They one and all halted between two alternatives. They one and all tried to avoid an outright choice. All tried to ride the fence.[8]

The Anabaptists, apart from a lunatic fringe group, were not anti-government. They were law-abiding citizens. They did not deny the secular government had both the responsibility and authority to rule and govern society nor were they unwilling to submit to the authority of secular government. Their fight was over the right of government to rule their conscience in religious matters. They said, "You have no right to use the steel sword to force me to have my child baptized."

The basic difference between the Anabaptists and both the Reformers and the Roman Catholics was the true nature of the _ekklesia._ In the case of the Anabaptists, they insisted on defining the _ekklesia_ as an organism that you entered by spiritual birth. However, in the Reformer's and Roman Catholic's view, you could be a member of two different _ekklesias._ You were in the 'visible' _ekklesia_ of Christ by being part of the 'Christian' nation or Christian home. If you were born in a Catholic country then you were baptized a

---

[8] Leonard Verduin, _The Reformers and Their Stepchildren_ (The Christian Hymnary Publishers, Sarasota, Florida, 1991 reprint) 16-17.

Catholic. If you were born in a Lutheran or Presbyterian country then you were baptized a Lutheran or Presbyterian. If you were born again and a true believer in Christ then you were also a member of the invisible *ekklesia* made up of all the elect.

The Anabaptists objected to the fence riding and insisted that there was one *ekklesia* of Christ and it was made up of only true believers who had been born again. The refusal of the Anabaptist to have their children baptized in the state church was sufficient grounds to put them to death. A denial of the authority over the conscience by the 'visible' church approved by the state was viewed as a sin against both Christ and the stability of the nation itself. There was only one church and it was the state church.

We do not have time to go into to all the problems created by the wedding of church and state. My only point here is to demonstrate that most of the blood shed by both Catholics and the Reformers was brought about by the logical application of an unbiblical doctrine of the *ekklesia* of Christ. The national, visible, state *ekklesia* was the only *ekklesia*. There was no being a part of Christ unless you were part of the visible national *ekklesia*. Unfortunately, this very bad view of *ekklesia* was continued by the Reformers themselves. When they killed Catholics and Anabaptists they were consistently following their conscience and their theology of the church. Unfortunately their conscience was trained with a very defective doctrinal view of the *ekklesia*. They never left the Roman Catholic view of the *ekklesia*.

As noted earlier, the 'visible/invisible' and 'local/universal' view of *ekklesia* was first posited by the Reformers. The Roman Catholics hated any idea of an 'invisible' church. They would have agreed one hundred percent with Landmark Baptists on that point.

William Cunningham rightly emphasizes that when Rome entered into controversy with the Reformers, Rome always wanted to start the discussion by defining the church. Rome felt she could win the argument of the 'true church' since she pretended to be able to trace her institutional existence back to Saint Peter and Christ. Once you agree that "Christ established one true church on earth" then Rome appears to have a good case for making the claim that she is that church. When you start tracing the true institutional church to which, supposedly, *"Christ has given his authority on earth,"* then some of Rome's arguments seem convincing. Begin by insisting that the *ekklesia* Christ established is a spiritual organism which is entered only by the new birth, and it is a different ball game.

The primary reason Rome wants to start the argument regarding the nature of the church is the clear implication as it relates to authority. If Christ has indeed 'established' a church, meaning institution, and I can identify that church today, then all further discussion on any subject relating to the church or Christianity is totally governed by that true church. Everyone must recognize and submit to that one true church that Christ has established and given the authority to speak for him. We must listen to and obey Christ by listening to and obeying what his church says. In other words, the real question is authority. I am sure you can see that both Rome and the Landmark Baptists use the identical arguments about authority to prove they are the one true church. Cunningham has stated it well:

...were the views which they [Rome] generally propound on the general subject of the church, and their application to the Church of Rome [or a Landmark Baptist], established, this would supersede all further discussion of individual doctrines; for the practical result of them is virtually to put the Church in the room of God as the immediate revealer of all truth, as well as the dispenser of all grace, or at least to put the Church in the room of his Word as the only standard of faith,—and the conclusion, of course, is, that men should implicitly submit their understandings to whatever the church may promulgate to them.[9]

This reminds me of the conversation between a Roman Catholic and a Protestant neighbor:

Protestant: "Exactly what do you believe?"

Roman Catholic: "I believe what the church believes."

Prot: "And what does the church believe?"

RC: "It believes what I believe."

Prot: "And exactly what do both you and the church believe?"

RC: "We both believe the same thing."

I can remember many occasions discussing the gospel with a Roman Catholic priest. All would go well until we would come to a Scripture, usually in Hebrews, that he just could not handle. I would ask him, "What do you honestly think that verse means?" He would smile, close the Bible, and say, "John, the real difference between you and me in our beliefs is the question of authority. My church, instituted by Christ, tells me what that verse means and you

---

[9] William Cunningham, *Historical Theology, A Review of the Principal Doctrinal Discussions in the Christian Church Since the Apostolic Age* Vol. 1 (Edinburg, T. and T. Clark, MDCCCLXIII) 9, 10.

think you have the right to understand it on your own." The name of the game is authority and liberty of conscience.

It is essential to see what Rome was actually teaching. We can only understand the Reformers on this subject as we see the specific arguments to which they were responding.

"The substance of Romish doctrine upon this subject is that Christ has established on earth the church as a distinct society, which is not only to continue always indefectible [meaning incapable of having any flaws] or without ceasing to exist, but to stand out visibly...not liable to error, but will always continue to promulgate the truth, and the truth alone." [10]

Rome's first shot was aimed at destroying any foundation except itself as the final authority. This was their first argument:

Where there is not a valid ministry, there is no true church. Protestants have not a valid ministry, and therefore they are not a true church.[11]

You can see how your definition of _ekklesia_ determines everything. The Landmark Baptist says, "Amen," but he insists his church, instead of the Roman Catholic, is the one true church that Christ established. The Landmark Baptist, like Rome, is the only church to which Christ has given authority to baptize and organize churches. All other baptisms are 'alien baptisms.' If you have no 'valid ministry,' one that has been given authority by the one true Church that Christ established on earth, then the next step, which Rome readily took, was to believe there could be no salvation outside their church because there is no

---

[10] Ibid., 10.

[11] Ibid., 11.

authorized individual to dispense the holy sacraments of grace.

You can see how the idea of 'valid ministry' became a pivotal issue. What gives any ministry validity before God and before man? Who alone has the authority to establish or verify that a given ministry is truly valid? The Roman Church, and most Protestants want to locate the source of authority in the church, and since an unseen invisible church cannot give visible authority it follows it must be the local or visible church that alone can give authority. Any ministry not authorized or validated by the church that Christ authorized cannot be of God. One thing is certain, the moment you start discussing the subject of authority, the institutionalist is ready to denounce the invisible church and insist on only a local church.

The real problem is not separating the so-called 'universal' church from the so-called 'local' church. That particular argument is really only an outgrowth of another and more serious difference. The real error is thinking of the church *only* in purely institutional terms instead of seeing it as redeemed people who are all bound together in Christ whether they act like it or not. The church surely has clearly defined institutional functions and responsibilities, but that is not the primary emphasis in the New Testament Scriptures.

Every duty enjoined on a believer in the New Testament Scriptures is always based on the fact that he is joined to Christ and therefore joined to every other believer. No one is urged to any given behavior toward another believer because they both 'joined the same local church.' The exhortation is always because both are members of the 'body of Christ.'

The real danger in institutionalizing the church is the view of authority that must inevitably follow. Instead of being a *means* of grace the church soon becomes the *agent* of grace. The next step makes the 'ordained clergy' to be the only people 'duly authorized' to dispense that grace. It is impossible for such a view to keep the church from becoming an *essential* intermediary between God and the souls of men and women.

B.B. Warfield has put this point in focus. He shows that there are only two basic views one can take of the nature and authority of the church. The first is Romanism and the other is biblical. This is the difference between sacerdotalism and evangelicalism. The basic difference is the way God brings his saving grace into a soul. Does God work upon men immediately or does he only deal with men through appointed (duly authorized) instrumentalities, namely, a visible, 'true' church with appointed (duly authorized) elders or priests? Is the primary concern to have the right institutional church order and authority structure, or is the primary concern seeing the marks of the work of the Holy Spirit in the personal experience of individuals? How do we judge what is a 'true church'?

I suggest that you check the view held by your church and pastor with the two views set forth by Warfield in the following quote and see whether you are biblical or Romish:

> The issue concerns the immediacy of the saving operations of God: Does God save men by immediate operations of his grace upon their souls, or does he act upon them only through

the medium of instrumentation [the local church] established for that purpose?[12]

This is the heart of the institutionalist's theology. The visible organization is the only God-ordained agency with 'authority' to do God's work on earth, and the elders, or priests, are the only duly authorized leaders to rule that agency. This Roman rubbish is accepted whenever you totally institutionalize the church as many are doing today. Warfield continues:

> The typical form of sacerdotalism is supplied by the teaching of the Church of Rome. In that teaching the church is held to be the institution of salvation, through which alone is salvation conveyed to men. Outside the church and its ordinances salvation is not supposed to be found; grace is communicated by and through the ministrations of the church, otherwise not. The two maxims are therefore in force: **where the church is, there is the Spirit; outside the church there is no salvation…**[13]

Let me give the above quotation again and substitute the word "authority" for the word "salvation" and see whether it fits your view of authority. The emphasis is mine.

The typical form of sacerdotalism is supplied by the teaching of the Church of Rome. In that teaching the church is held to be the **only institution given authority** by Christ, it is through the church **[visible/local]** alone that **authority** is conveyed to men. Outside the church and its ordinances **authority** is not supposed to be found; **authority** is communicated by and through the ministrations of the **[visible/local]** church, otherwise not. The two maxims are

---

[12] B. B. Warfield, *The Plan of Salvation* (Fig-Books.com, 2013) 6.

[13] Ibid.

therefore in force: **Where the Church is, there is Christ's authority; outside the [local] church there is no authority ...**

I am sure we can see that many Baptist churches have a Roman Catholic view of authority! It amazes me that men who will repudiate Rome's doctrine of exclusive salvation will still hold rigidly to Rome's system of exclusive church authority when both things rest on the same premise. Let us continue with Warfield:

> Over against this whole view evangelicalism...sweeps away every intermediary between the soul and its God, and leaves the soul dependent for its salvation on God alone, operating upon it by his immediate grace. ... In direct opposition to the maxims of consistent sacerdotalism, he takes therefore as his mottoes: **Where the Spirit is, there is the Church; outside the body of saints there is no salvation.**"[14]

A consistent institutionalist must demand far more than the presence of the Holy Spirit applying the truth of saving grace in order to accept a group of people as 'a true NT church' or as a valid mission work born of God's Spirit. He must see that work under the direct authority of a local church. Some men will also insist on a correct creed, the right officers, proper procedure, precise worship format, etc. The basic assumptions of a true institutionalist are far closer to those of Rome than they are to the evangelicalism of the New Testament Scriptures. Certain groups of sincere believers in Christ may be considered real Christians, but they are merely a 'religious organization.' They are not a 'church of Christ' until they obey God by following his clearly revealed (in our books and history) church order. A

---

[14] Ibid.

mission work or para-church ministry may *appear* to be blessed of God but it definitely has not been established by Christ's orders unless it is under the authority of a local church. A Baptist missionary paper recently illustrated this view when stating, "If a man is called of God to preach the Word, he must never allow himself to be severed from the body of Christ. Only within the church will he find the experience, guidance, and support to fulfill his calling. Apart from the church he has no calling from the Lord of the church."

This author has totally confused the 'body of Christ' with a 'local congregation.' He is talking like a Roman Catholic. You can be severed from a local church without being severed from the 'body of Christ.' This statement reveals the root error in the typical Reformed Baptist doctrine of the 'local' church. We dare not take the properties of the body of Christ (which is always singular and is synonymous with 'the elect') and apply those properties to a local congregation. The above author is saying that the thousands of believers (including William Carey, Hudson Taylor, etc.) who have gone to the mission field under an interdenominational mission board were never called by 'the Lord of the church' simply because they were not under the authority of a local church. This is the Roman Catholic view of authority.

In this Roman view, the only criterion that establishes who is truly called of God is the individual's relationship to the authority vested in the local church. This mentality cannot help but treat the local church as Christ's true and only vicar on earth. Since this view usually insists that the 'authority' is in the elders (often only one, the pastor), the end result means the pastor is Christ's vicar. In such a system the 'lord of the church' is really the pastor.

The New Testament Scriptures will not allow us to separate the work of the Spirit and the church of Christ in this way, but the institutionalist is often forced to do this very thing. It is local church order and authority that concerns him. He is more concerned with the 'church' (institution) than he is with the obvious and genuine work of the Holy Spirit (the reality of God's presence in people).

In the eyes of the institutionalist, the worst sins are those that challenge the 'duly authorized' forms, ceremonies, traditions, or leadership of 'Christ's duly authorized church.' It does not matter how powerfully the Holy Spirit of God is applying the truth to hearts, the institutionalist only recognizes the outward form and order. It is easy to see why an institutionalist must become a legalist regardless of how hard he tries to avoid it. What the Scriptures call love and tolerance, the institutionalist must view as compromise with clear truth (his system). It is tragic but true. It is tragic because some great and godly men have sincerely shed their blood and destroyed churches over secondary principles and thought they were doing God a favor even while they swung the sword in 'holy zeal' for the 'cause of truth.'

An illustration of the inability of the institutionalist to accept the work of God's Spirit outside the 'duly authorized' local church was the 'scandal' created by George Whitfield when he had communion in the open field and many pastors from various denominational backgrounds helped to serve it. Thousands attended and revival took place in the fields but many said, "It cannot be of God," because it was not under the control and authority of any institutional church. A true institutionalist had no choice but to denounce Whitfield and refuse to have anything to do with his 'free lance' ministry. Would to God that he would raise up some more freelance rebels like Whitfield and William Carey in our day. John Bunyan was hated and denounced by the Baptists because he refused to make baptism necessary for church communion. Baptist publishers are still condemning his article "Differences in Judgment About Water Baptism No Bar To Communion."

If you had been a hostage several years ago in Iran and once a month all of the Christians had been allowed to get together for one hour, would you have considered it proper to take bread and wine and have a remembrance service of the blessed Savior? Or would you have refused because some of those participating had never been immersed? Would you have insisted that the *Lord's* Table is really the *local church's* table and since this group of believers was not a 'duly authorized' church you therefore could not participate? Would such a service be un-biblical if there had been no 'ordained elder' present to 'consecrate' the elements?

Some institutionalists cringe at the clear implications of their position when it is worked out in real life, but the true institutionalist will say without shame, "Amen!" I might say that the latter is the one being honest with his presuppositions. All 'true' Reformed Baptists hold that there is no authority outside the local church. They would never say there is no *salvation* outside the church, but their basic mentality and view of *authority* is Roman Catholic. As already mentioned, all you have to do is replace the word *salvation* with the word *authority* in the quotation from

Warfield and you have the view vehemently preached and practiced by many Baptists today. Often I have heard young zealots denounce what appeared to be a real movement of God's Spirit simply because the group or man was not 'under the authority of a local church.' If Christ established a clear institutional role model church, then the young zealots may be correct and I am fighting against God's clear truth in this book. However, if...

Chapter Three
Views of Authority

The theme of this chapter on the *ekklesia* deals with authority. This is the main issue in nearly all discussions of the *ekklesia* of Christ. Several years ago a group of Reformed Baptist pastors published a book entitled *Shepherding God's Flock*. The book was specifically aimed at trying to correct a growing problem of abusive eldership within that movement. The very fact the book was written and published is testimony to the severity of the problem about which these men were concerned. It is obvious that there are a lot of elders in that movement, and in other movements, who are acting like mini-popes. These writers evidently felt a moral obligation to the church to expose such tyranny. The introduction says it all:

> The failure of God's office bearers to exercise biblical rule in his church in the past has certainly led to confusion, impurity, and doctrinal laxity. On the other hand, the abuse of power by some shepherds of the flock is a present reality that has sometimes produced tragic fruits. Among these are beaten and scarred believers who feel themselves forced to leave local churches, immaturity and dependency among believers who remain in those churches, a lock-step uniformity which undermines genuine Christian liberty, and a siege mentality toward any questioning or criticism from the outside.[15]

---

[15] Roger O. Beardmore, ed., *Shepherding God's Flock* (Harrisonburg, VA, Sprinkle Publications, year of publication not stated) 9.

No good purpose would be served by naming the individuals against whom *Shepherding God's Flock* was written. Those within the Reformed Baptist movement will know the major characters (and devotees) who are being rebuked. Those outside that movement will probably be able to identify the same symptoms in men within their own denomination or movement.

The book has one great weakness. None of the authors in the book make any attempt to trace the problem to a root cause. They have purposely kept the theme of the book to one subject, namely the abuse of eldership. How and why that abusive attitude came into being, was nurtured, and allowed to grow is not discussed. All of the authors treat the tyrants against whom they are writing as aberrations of their own doctrine of eldership. We would suggest that it is possible that the tyrants are in reality the logical conclusion to that very view of eldership and as long as the same system of eldership is maintained tyrannical men will continue to arise in their midst. Again, the introduction says it all:

> It is not the purpose of this book to debate the institution of the eldership as such, but simply to explore the claims and the limits of the authority of elders. Its intended goal is not to break new doctrinal ground, but rather to probe the more practical aspects of the doctrines of church government already established and commonly held.[16]

The moment I read that statement I knew the book would have a very limited effect and would do very little to solve the real problems. I knew it was 'surface' treatment. I confess I was surprised at the statement because I knew all

---

[16] Ibid., 11.

of the contributing authors. I knew they were men that took doctrine seriously. They also believed that correct doctrine led to correct living and bad doctrine led to bad living. I was amazed that they had totally jettisoned that conviction in this book. They were saying, "Our doctrine is correct, the problem is with the 'practical' application." I would suggest that it was the doctrine of eldership believed and taught by the Reformed Baptists that gave birth to and nourished the very problem they were trying to solve. It is the purpose of this book to go one step further and discuss some basic presuppositions that I believe must be changed before the problem can be solved. A large part of the Reformed Baptist movement is still following the very man against whom *Shepherding God's Flock* was written.

Some Reformed Baptists, as well as others, have attempted to wed two things that are totally opposite. These men have tried to put elements of Presbyterianism into a semi-Baptist framework and managed to destroy the strengths of both systems and exaggerate the weakness of both systems. Both the concept of Presbyterian rule through eldership and the Baptist rule by congregationalism have great strengths when applied in their own settings. However, those very same strengths become very dangerous when they are put into another system. It is this fact that helps to explain the problem of abusive eldership in the circles addressed in *Shepherding God's Flock*. Let me explain what I mean as it concerns authority and eldership.

PRESBYTERIAN ELDERSHIP

First, we will look at the Presbyterian view of eldership.

(1) In this system, the authority of the church is in the eldership and not the congregation. It is for this reason that

a Presbyterian congregation cannot hold an official congregational meeting without an elder being present.

(2) In a Presbyterian church, the pastor does not join the local church nor is he subject to the discipline of the local church. The pastor is received by, and is a member of, the Presbytery (the pastors and elders in a given area) and is subject to the discipline of the Presbytery and not the local church.

The checks and balances in this system make it very difficult for a pastor to act as a pope. This system of eldership works very well until the Presbytery goes bad. When that happens everything is lost and the local church is hostage to the Presbytery because the authority is in the Presbytery and not the local congregation. The Presbytery has the final authority to approve or disapprove who will pastor a church in their Presbytery in that system of government. True, the Presbytery cannot force a congregation to accept a pastor they do not want, but the Presbytery can refuse to receive a pastor that a congregation does want. The congregation either bows to the authority of the Presbytery or is forced to withdraw from the denomination.

The Presbyterian system of authority has some very good features. If several families in a Presbyterian congregation feel the pastor is not teaching the truth or if his behavior is hurting the church, they can go and talk to him. If they cannot convince him he is wrong, or if he refuses to listen to them, they can lodge a complaint against him in Presbytery and he will have to answer it whether he wants to or not. In other words, the pastor is subject to other pastors and elders. He is not a law unto himself. Presbyterianism can usually handle and resolve local church fights much better than Baptist congregationalism. This is especially true when the trouble involves the pastor or his authority. The checks and balances of power work well as long as the Presbytery is made up of godly men.

BAPTIST ELDERSHIP

Second, let us look at the Baptist system of authority. Historically, Baptists have taken the congregational form of government. They have resisted both the idea of a Presbytery beyond the local church and putting the final authority of the local church into the office of eldership. Baptist congregations in the past have had elders, but always those elders were subject to the rule of the congregation. The pastor and elders functioned as leaders of the congregation, and as such, their views (rightly so) have great influence. But *ultimately*, the congregation chose whether or not to accept the recommendations of the pastor and elders. It is at this point that some present-day Baptists (mostly Reformed Baptists) have departed from both the Bible and their Baptist forefathers. They have adopted the Presbyterian view of eldership and put the authority of the church in the hands of the eldership, thereby rejecting congregational rule. However, they have also rejected the idea of a Presbytery, or any authority, beyond the local church. They have destroyed the checks and balances established by the Presbytery. This is a hybrid view of authority of recent origin. It is really 'Baptist' Catholicism. The evils that *Shepherding God's Flock* is fighting are the 'good and necessary consequences' of such a mixture of contrary principles.

Here is the problem in this hybrid system: (1) If the authority of a local church is in the eldership and not the congregation (Presbyterian eldership), and (2) if there is no authority past the local congregation (Baptist congregationalism), then (3) to whom can an appeal be made when an elder acts like a tyrant? In such a situation, the eldership is a law unto itself with no accountability to anyone but its own conscience! In such a system, if several families come to the pastor with a sincere concern and he either refuses to listen or is not convinced that they are correct, those individuals are not allowed to even talk to another person after they leave his office. To do so is to be 'guilty of rebellion against God's duly authorized leadership.' Such a system is nothing but Roman popery. There is no check and balance because the eldership is ultimately responsible to no one but itself. A tyrant can have a field day and be untouchable in such a system.

As previously mentioned, either the Presbyterian view of authority or the Baptist view of authority will work very well. The object of this article is not to state which view is biblical or preferable. I have long believed that a combination of the two would be the best. However, a hybrid system that adopts a Presbyterian view of eldership and then denies *both* congregationalism and a Presbytery has, even if unknowingly, created an eldership that has all of the unchecked authority of an infallible pope. Eldership rule without a Presbytery is Roman Catholicism. Someone has made the following observations:

1.   A good man in a bad system will not abuse the bad system.

2. A good system can deal with a bad man and curtail his power.

3. A bad system attracts, encourages, and protects bad men.

The last mentioned situation (3) is the case with the authority system taught and practiced by many Baptists, especially Reformed Baptists, today. This system has no way to deal with tyrants. Its basic foundation of authority makes the tyrant untouchable. The congregation is powerless to remedy the problem because the 'authority is in' the eldership,' and sister churches are forced to 'mind their own business' and not infringe on the 'autonomy' of the local church since there is no 'authority past the local church.' Christ's suffering sheep are either forced to 'vote with their feet' and leave the church they love, or to remain and endure continued abuse from the tyrannical leadership. Neither option is pleasant. Little wonder that the evils mentioned in *Shepherding God's Flock* so often occur in such a system, and as I mentioned before, will continue to occur until the system is changed. It is impossible to take some elements of Presbyterianism (rule by elders) but reject the concept of a Presbytery (as a check on elders) without creating a framework with the potential for the very problems addressed by the authors of *Shepherding God's Flock.*

The men who have created this hybrid system of authority, or who presently hold to it, must either (1) return to Baptist congregationalism, or (2) form some kind of Presbytery. Until they do one or the other, any movement using this hybrid view will experience a continual repetition of the evils that *Shepherding God's Flock* so forcefully and accurately condemns.

Can you imagine what our country would be like if the President was not subject to Congress or Congress was not subject to the Supreme Court? Most people do not realize that the success of our form of government is the fact it is built foursquare on the belief that man is a sinner who cannot be trusted with authority. The system of checks and balances was deliberately established to check man's lust for power and authority. Our founders believed the old saying, "Power corrupts, and absolute power corrupts absolutely."

A clear illustration of the truth I am trying to establish is the Reformed Baptist Missions Services established by some Reformed Baptist pastors several years ago. The Reformed Baptist movement was greatly stymied for a long time, by its own admission, because of their view of missions and the local church. They totally rejected 'mission boards' and insisted that only an individual local church could send out a missionary. If a church was too small to be able to do that then the individual wanting to go to the mission field would move his membership into a larger church and the smaller church would funnel their money through the big church. Because some of these Reformed Baptist pastors were godly men and had a real heart for missions they were not satisfied with the total ineffectiveness of this system. They have never publicly repudiated the system but they have repudiated it in practice.

It was in this atmosphere that the Reformed Baptist Missions Services was born. It is a separate organization with its own constitution and budget. This was forbidden under the original Reformed Baptists' doctrine of the local church. The organization meets once a year and sets its agenda and committees, etc. Member churches send delegates to the yearly meeting where the business is handled. Local churches may join RBMS by being approved by a vote of the RBMS members and paying a yearly fee. The RBMS can likewise discipline a local church out of membership at the annual business meeting. Several years ago they disciplined a church out of their organization over a wrong view of the Sabbath.

This missions effort seems to be working very well. However, no one seems ready to publicly admit that the primary reason it is working is that it *operates exactly like a Presbytery* and has, in practice, repudiated the idea that a single local church must own and control every ministry. For all practical purposes the RBMS is a Presbytery. Its decisions cannot be challenged by anyone.

We should add a word here about church splits and abuse of authority. Most of the time when a church splits over a leader's tyrannical attitude, the new group, like the book mentioned above, will not question the doctrine of eldership but will automatically establish the very same system of eldership. They merely get new elders. It is sad but true that the same attitude will soon be found in the new elders. We can wonder if the leaders of the split were really opposed to the system of tyranny or merely upset because they were not the ones in charge of running the show. How many church splits occur because, "If I can't be the big frog in the pond, I will build my own pond"?

Three Views of Authority

There are three basic views of authority, or government, with many degrees in between. This is just as true in the religious world as it is in the secular world. We will examine these three one at a time.

1. THE DICTATORSHIP

First, there is the **dictator.** One man alone is the pope, general, president, or whatever. That person's word is law on the basis of the strength and authority of his 'office.' He is the undisputed, 'duly authorized' leader. The individual's authority is not directly related to his ability or his character. He totally controls his kingdom either by raw power (guns, money, fear,) or by masterful manipulation of other people. He may be ignorant or intelligent, wicked or godly, kind or mean, but he is still the 'boss' because he occupies the office. The following are always present in this system:

(1) There is always a chain of command or 'pecking order.' An individual's authority is measured entirely by where he is in the chain of command. In the army it is the general, colonel, captain, etc. In religion it is the pope, cardinal, bishop, etc., or else the pastor, elder, deacon, etc. The offices are often used as 'carrot sticks' to reward the faithful and control the dissenters. The offices, or positions of power, are bought and paid for by unquestioning obedience to every whim of the top man.

(2) The offices are filled from the top down and never from the bottom up. Only the present leaders can bring someone else into leadership. There may be a mock election but only those approved by the top can even be considered as a candidate. The church congregation with this view of authority does not really elect its officers any more than the enlisted men in the army choose their officers. The congregation may, in some cases, be allowed to ratify the

people chosen by the pastor or elders but it is merely a formality.

(3) The authority is always in the office and often has little or nothing to do with either the ability or character of the individual. A general who is an idiot has as much authority as a genius. The pope or pastor has the full 'authority of his office' regardless of whether he is capable or not. Rome is not the only religious organization with egg on its face because of either stupidity or tyranny being 'clothed with Divine authority.' *Shepherding God's Flock* gives ample proof that this tragic fact still exists today.

(4) There are never any checks or balances over leadership in this system. The 'God-ordained' individual is 'duly authorized' by God and is answerable to no one else. The king is king by 'divine right.' The general speaks the last word simply because he is the general. The pastor is the bishop of your soul and is accountable to God for your well-being. This 'God-ordained' responsibility gives him not only the *right* but the *responsibility* to totally run your life—*for your own good* of course! The more 'sincere' the leader is in his imagined 'duty to God,' the more tyrannical he is likely to become. He not only has the 'authority,' but he also has the 'awesome responsibility to God' to 'guide' (control) your life. Of course, he does it only because he loves you and is concerned for 'your own good.' The 'lay' people are duty bound to obey God's 'duly authorized leader' *even if he is wrong*, and God will '*reward your obedience.*' I have heard that papal nonsense preached from Reformed Baptist pulpits!

The typical example of this same form of authority in the secular world is found in the army. Can you imagine telling a Roman army officer that if he really wants to be great he should become a 'servant of his men'? In Matthew 20:26-27, Jesus is giving us the essence of the world's view of authority. It is 'lording it over the conscience.' The New Testament concept of authority is totally contradictory to the chain of command and 'the authority is in the office' concept. The consistent religious example of this pagan form of authority is the Roman Catholic Church. Can you imagine telling the pope that he is no more infallible than the underlings who call him 'Holy Father'? Could the pope ever be convinced that allowing men to kneel down and kiss his ring is nothing short of blasphemy and could never be biblically looked upon as act of 'submission to Christ's duly authorized authority'? There are pastors today who would not demand you kneel and kiss a ring, but they do that very thing in another form. They demand you do not question either what they say or do or their right to be a law unto themselves.

Notice the similarity between the secular and religious forms of this view of authority as follows:

The line of separation between the 'officers and enlisted men' (clergy and laity) is the first step toward the Gentile (secular) and religious, as illustrated in Roman Catholicism, view of authority. This will stifle and destroy the priesthood of believers. When a man demands that he be called by a special title to constantly remind people of his 'holy office' (and authority), that individual is infected with the Roman view of authority. In no sense am I saying that it is wrong to call someone 'pastor.' It is probably a good thing to teach children to say 'pastor' in the same sense that we call our physician 'doctor.' However, if this is *demanded* or ever done for the *same reason* that an army officer is called 'sir' and is saluted, then we have totally departed from the concept of authority taught by our Savior. We have become Romanist and are practicing priestcraft. We actually mean 'father' when we say 'pastor' under those circumstances. See Matthew 23:8-12.

In my pastorates I was called "Pastor John" and that usually wound up "PJ." That did not bother me in the least and I never thought I was allowing 'God's holy office' to be slandered. Many of the men called me "John." Paul was never called "Reverend Paul" or "Pastor Paul." Some men today demand that they be called "Pastor" despite the fact that the great Apostle was content with plain "Paul" or "Brother Paul." This attitude reveals one of the marked differences between true and false shepherds. If you want to be ruggedly biblical and follow Scripture you will never demand that anyone call you reverend or pastor.

I am sure we can see that whenever the authority is put into the office you are moving toward a dictator type of leadership. Such a system can easily ignore personal qualities and emphasize only the institutional structure. It is impossible to develop and utilize spiritual gifts within the 'laity' when this view is in control of the church. There are only two gifts in any church that accepts this view. A giant tongue, the preacher, speaks and a giant ear, the congregation, obediently listens without question.

2. TOTAL DEMOCRACY

The second form of authority is the exact opposite of the dictator. It is pure and **total democracy**. This system will wind up in 'mob rule' and destroy itself or it will get so sick of anarchy that it will 'elect' a dictator. Someone has jokingly tried to use Acts 19:32 to prove that the early church must have been independent Baptist because this passage portrays a Baptist business meeting. It many cases it would not be too far from the truth. In the system of total democracy no one is supposed to have any 'authority.' No one is 'officially' functioning as a leader, I say 'officially' because every group, including the cows and pigs in the barnyard, has a pecking order. In this scenario the church is organized as a giant committee and settles everything around a table (preferably *round*). Everyone has equal authority. There is no 'one man ministry' nor is there any 'office' that has 'authority.' All of the attempts that I have ever seen to carry out this idea have wound up with clearly recognized 'unofficial' popes and a rigid but 'unofficial' pecking order. The Plymouth Brethren denomination is a classic illustration of this system. Every secular dictatorship and every religious cult started out with this 'ideal' in mind. The results were inevitable.

I remember seeing a cartoon with a group of men sitting around a table. One man had a crown on his head and was sitting on a large throne. This man was saying, "The round table shows that we are all equal. The throne I am sitting on and the crown on my head means that I am just a tad more equal." Orwell's *Animal Farm* is far more evident in religious circles than in political ones.

The Old and New Testaments, as well as church history, clearly demonstrate that God gives some men the gifts necessary for leadership. It is the responsibility of those men to be willing to serve in leadership roles and it is the responsibility of the congregation to recognize those leaders and follow them. Second Chronicles 12:32 is a classic text on authority.

3. REPRESENTATIVE GOVERNMENT

The third form of authority is **elected leadership** acting as representatives of those who elected them. In both the secular and religious world this principle is worked out in many different ways. The United States, England, Germany, France, etc., are all democracies but they have different systems of representation. Most Protestant denominations use some form of representative government. Both Baptist and Presbyterian leadership begin with the local congregation electing its representatives. From that point on there is a great difference in how authority is worked out.

The obvious question is, "What do the Scriptures say?" Our answer will always be determined by our basic presuppositions concerning the nature and function of the church. The New Testament Scriptures are not abundantly clear on this subject. The apostles do not give us a role model institutional church. It gives us basic principles. Neither a Roman Catholic nor a Puritan would view leadership and authority in the *ekklesia* of Christ the same way an Anabaptist would. Rome believes that Christ 'founded a church' and endowed it with the authority to be his sole representative on earth. Outside of that church there is neither salvation nor authority. The Pope, as the head of the Roman system, is Christ's vicar on earth. The man in control, the pope, regardless of who he may be, is infallible in his pronouncements and is responsible to no human authority. He has this authority purely on the grounds of his office. Whenever we view the church primarily as an *institution* endowed with exclusive authority because it has been 'duly authorized and constituted' by God, we have already taken the first step toward the Roman Catholic view of authority.

We simply must maintain a view of the church of Christ that sees it as first a *spiritual* organism and not just a physical organization. As mentioned in a previous chapter, it is not without significance that Rome hated the doctrine of the 'invisible' church and vehemently argued that there was no church except the 'visible' church. It amazes me that all Landmark Baptists, and many Reformed Baptists, follow Rome's view of 'local' (visible) church authority. There needs to be a lot of work done on this subject. Let me sketch a few broad categories.

(1) Both the membership in a congregation and the individual's relationship with the leaders must be based on mutual consent. Our only weapons or bands that bind people are truth and love.

(2) There should *always* be a plurality of leadership to avoid the ever-present danger of popery.

(3) Leaders must be accountable to someone besides themselves. Every human being should be responsible in some way to other human beings. This is not possible if we reject *both* congregationalism and a Presbytery. To reject both of these things is to literally create an untouchable pope and make real accountability impossible.

(4) However, plurality and *equality* are two different things. Equality of eldership is a figment of idealistic imagination. Every congregation has *one* pastor whether it admits to that fact or not. Every group, whether in the secular world, the religious world, or in the animal barnyard has a 'pecking order.' A congregation with two 'equal' pastors is like a wife with two husbands.

The pastor's submission to both the church and the other elders is in no way contrary to what I just said. Likewise, the pastor being the spiritual leader is not inconsistent with his being under human authority. A true pastor is both the leader and a servant at the same time. There is equality of eldership in that the pastor gets *one vote* in the elder's meeting. If he gets outvoted, then he submits. However, there is not equality in ministry and gifts, especially in preaching. Likewise, each elder does not get equal time every time he disagrees with something the pastor preached. The preaching pastor exerts by far the most influence in a congregation but must not have any more raw authority than anyone else.

(5) One man being recognized and accepted as the pastor in no way destroys the priesthood of believers. We strongly affirm that every believer is a priest before God and called to minister with the pastor. However, their respective ministries are not the same. Every believer is not a preacher any more than every pastor is an apostle. The 'priesthood of *believers'* must not become the 'priesthood of *preachers.'* The fact that all believers are priests *before God* does not mean that all believers are leaders *before men.*

We must never equate the many exhortations concerning duties to one another with nothing but public ministry to the congregation in the stated meetings of the church. Every single believer is to exhort and encourage every other believer, including exhorting (and don't forget encouraging) the pastor, but that does not mean that they stand up in the Sunday morning church service and exhort "Uncle Billy to quit cheating on his wife" or encourage "Aunt Minnie to keep trusting the Lord even though she, and everyone else, knows what Uncle Billy is doing." Most of the duties enjoined in the 'one-anothering' passages are private. Do not equate public preaching and 'one-anothering.' Also do not, as many preachers do, think the elder is exempt from the 'one-another' passages. Only some believers have the gifts and responsibility for preaching, but every believer has the ability and the responsibility for 'one-anothering.'

Every member of every assembly should feel a duty to tell fellow believers, including the elders, "You are wrong" when it is obvious that is the case. If a sincere Christian either feels that is not his duty or he is too afraid of the elder to be honest with him, something is terribly wrong with that assembly.

(6) Two things should greatly help determine a given pastor's duties: (1) his own peculiar gifts (and weaknesses), and (2) the needs and strengths of the particular congregation that he pastors. The same man may well have some different duties in different situations. A congregation with few, if any, capable teachers or leaders (because it is either new or untrained), will require things of a pastor that a congregation with many capable and mature leaders will not require. It is not biblical to define 'official pastoral duty and authority' with an 'office' concept regardless of either peculiar gifts or situations. This is nothing but a Roman Catholic approach.

A pastor gifted in personal work and counseling, but not too adept at organization or administration, obviously should be freed to do what he is good at. Likewise, a pastor that has exceptional preaching gifts should be encouraged and allowed to exercise those gifts to Christ's church at large even if 'our congregation pays his salary.' This, of course, assumes that his ministry in the local church is causing that local situation to grow and that other people are helping in the responsibilities that would otherwise be neglected by his being away.

My point is that we dare not have a set procedure and definition of pastoral duties that is identical for all pastors and churches regardless of particular gifts and needs. Some churches would do well to hire a 'business manager' and literally forbid their pastor to in any way get involved with managing the business aspects of the church. They should also not allow such a pastor to be criticized for 'being away too much' if God is truly using him in helping other congregations and nothing is being neglected at home. In some cases, things in a local congregation would go a whole better if the pastor went away every Monday morning and did not return until Saturday evening!

Our concern should not be with *who* does what, but rather, *"Is everything that is necessary being taken care of in a satisfactory manner?"* Are we concerned that the work of God actually gets done or that only duly authorized elitists be allowed to do the work? In my mind, this is what plurality of leadership and the priesthood of all believers is all about. It is utilizing the gifts of all God's people to minister to as much of Christ's whole church as is possible.

(7) We must not confuse responsibility with authority or raw power. The NTS do not in any sense emphasize 'office and authority.' They speak of people, gifts, and responsibility. Eldership is not an office as much as it is a function, just as the church is more a spiritual organism than it is a physical institution. The church has distinct institutional functions, just as a pastor has 'official duties.'

However, when the emphasis is placed first on the 'institution' and the 'office,' we are starting at the wrong end. A leader that continually reminds us that he has 'authority' is really proving that he has no God-given authority at all. His constant exhortations to "submit to God's duly-authorized elder" prove that he is not a true leader of Christ's sheep. He is a thief who is attempting to drive the sheep away from Christ and draw them unto himself.

(8) A true leader has several clear marks. First, he has followers. Anyone who thinks he is a leader need only turn around and look if anyone is there. If no one is following, then the person is not a leader. However, that is not enough for the Christian. All leaders do not lead us in the same direction or to the same place. The test of a true Christian leader is whether he is first a follower himself and if he is following the right Person. A Christian leader cannot say, "Follow me," unless he finishes the statement, "*as I follow Christ.*" We dare not say, "Do this because I have authority to make you do it." We must say, "Do this because your Lord, in this text of Scripture, has commanded you." In one sense, we have no followers of ourselves. We are all followers of the Lamb. Leaders are merely pilgrims helping other pilgrims following the same Lord.

Unity and love are the things that make an assembly the closest thing to heaven we will ever experience on this earth. Where there is true, unified understanding of truth and a sincere love of each other, a congregation will bring honor and glory to their God and Savior. We should all pray for Acts 9:31 to be the experience of our congregations today.

Then had the churches rest throughout all Judaea and Galilee and Samaria, and were edified; and walking in the fear of the Lord, and in the comfort of the Holy Ghost, were multiplied.

Chapter Four
Incorrect Assumptions

Nearly every book I have read and every sermon I have heard on the subject 'The New Testament Church' made two dogmatic assumptions followed by a logical conclusion based upon those two assumptions. The two assumptions were not spelled out as clearly in each case, but always these two assumptions were treated as 'biblical facts' that were beyond either question or discussion. As a result, the view of the church was already established before you ever opened the Bible to discuss the subject. The implications flowing out of the conclusions were not always stated in bold terms, but again, all of the points were assumed to have been established unquestionably as biblical facts. These 'established facts' were then used as the key arguments to settle many difficult questions of church membership, of who may or may not partake of the Lord's Table, of which church is a 'true' church, etc.

ASSUMPTION NUMBER ONE: Jesus established a church on this earth and promised that this church would prevail in all ages. That 'fact' proves that there is a physical local church organization in the New Testament Scriptures given to us as a clear role model to be followed today in all of its details.

When I speak of 'a true NT church' in this book, it is this institutional role model concept that I am referring to. Those who make this assumption feel the very integrity and sufficiency of the Bible are at stake. In their minds, to reject this assumption is to reject the Bible as our complete rule of faith and practice, and believe that God has left us basically to 'do as we please' in church order. This assumption irrevocably commits you to a mindset toward the Scriptures that cannot avoid a sectarian and separatist attitude characterized by external legalism and tyrannical leadership.

ASSUMPTION NUMBER TWO: We can only expect God's blessing when we organize and operate our local church exactly like this 'true New Testament role model church.' We must follow the 'clear apostolic example' in its total function, its method of organization and operation, its officers, its membership requirements, etc., as they are clearly set forth in the Scriptures in every essential detail. I read an article on the church that began, 'We believe that simply a return to the biblical pattern of the church in a spirit of seeking the Lord with all of our hearts will bring the revival...'

CONCLUSION: To refuse to organize and operate the local congregation according to the role model given to us in Scripture by divine inspiration is to 'substitute man's wisdom for God's clearly revealed will.' This conclusion is inevitable when a sincere person adopts these two assumptions. He will more and more isolate himself from any individual or group that 'refuses to follow the true NT pattern for the church.' He will justify his actions by saying, "My conscience is bound to obey God's Word (clearly set forth in my creed). For me to have fellowship with any group or individual that deliberately refuses to submit to God's truth (my creed), is the same as my denying that God has spoken clearly on this matter." The very inspiration and authority of the Word of God is at stake in this man's mind. I readily admit that if the two assumptions are correct, then such a conclusion is valid. However, both assumptions are false.

It is a total waste of time to discuss any kind of organization or cooperation in the work of God's kingdom with a man committed to these two basic assumptions unless the particular work begins and ends with his specific 'local church.' It is all or nothing with him. One of his favorite expressions will be, "We cannot open the door to even the slightest exception to God's true church order." This person sees only two possible positions. (1) Admit that God's truth (his creed) cannot be violated by any exceptions, or else (2) admit that the Word of God is insufficient as a rule of practice for church order. The creed may be Baptist, Presbyterian, Lutheran, or even the 'no creed' creed of the Brethren, but the mentality and attitude toward other Christians will always be the same.

It ought to be obvious that such an approach to the doctrine of the church must soon lead to the attitude, spoken or unspoken, that "WE alone are the only people who really believe and follow all that the New Testament Scriptures teach about the church." Once this attitude is imbedded in the mind it does not take long to reason 'therefore we are **the true New Testament church**.' The arrogant pride and intolerance that attends such an attitude is an abomination to both God and men. No one thing has hindered the gospel of God's sovereign grace more than this attitude and mind set. History is full of bloodshed because men who held these presuppositions also acted upon the necessary implications whenever they had the civil or ecclesiastical power to do so.

It is impossible to make the first assumption without also making the second one. You cannot believe that the NTS reveal an institutional role model for church order as clearly as it teaches justification by faith without being forced to believe that we have all of the essential details of that model in our particular local church. Once this is believed, you have no choice but to claim divine authority for every detail of your particular system since God himself 'revealed that system in his inspired Word.' Likewise, you must then treat all who disagree with you as rebels that 'reject God's authority' because they 'refuse to bow to God's true church polity.'

I repeat: it is impossible to make the first assumption without finally coming to the logical conclusion that your system and organization is *the* true New Testament church. You may say that you are *a* true New Testament church, and that all who agree with you are also true New Testament churches, but the result will be basically the same in your attitude toward other believers. This kind of mind-set simply must lead to bigotry and conceit in order to be consistent with itself. You will only be able to enter into any kind of meaningful relationship and labor in the gospel with those who dot their *I*'s and cross their *T*'s exactly as you do. Even the slightest deviation must be seen as opening the door in compromise that in twenty years will erode and destroy everything.

We shall go into these assumptions in detail later; for now let me say that I reject both of these basic assumptions and the logical conclusions drawn from them. I believe this kind of reasoning forms the basic foundation of pure institutionalism, and institutionalism is the excuse that men of a certain temperament use to practice totalitarianism. Authority 'divinely vested' in either a man or an institution is Romanism, and it will always lead to the same totalitarian attitude expressed in that system. A man or an organization that sincerely believes they are 'duly authorized by God' to be his vicar will soon assume the right to control both the church as a whole and the conscience of every individual. I say without hesitation that I am an avowed opponent of papal authoritarian institutionalism regardless of whether it wears a Roman, Presbyterian, Baptist, Plymouth Brethren or any other robe. It is this error that produces tyrants for leaders and narrow-minded bigots as disciples. It has destroyed some good men and some great churches when every other weapon of Satan had failed.

Let me quickly state a few things that may be misunderstood. I believe, preach, and practice that every Christian should be a member of a local assembly and subject to its love and discipline. That does not mean an individual gives up either his liberty of conscience or his responsibility for using his gifts and talents as God leads him. In no sense am I downgrading the local assemblies of God's people. I have spent my life helping to establish and nurture congregations of God's people. Likewise, I am in no way opposed to a church having a doctrinal statement, constitution, order of worship, agreed procedures of operation, etc. Every group of people needs rules of order for the group's activities, and there must be agreement on those rules. All I am insisting on is that Scripture does not give us all of those rules, and we must therefore use our best judgment for the particular situation in which we find ourselves. We do not have, *and we do not need,* a proof text for everything in our constitution. We must follow every specific rule that God has given in his Word but we must also not add rules that he has not given.

I will never forget having breakfast with three Reformed Baptist brethren several years ago. They wanted to discuss the authority of the local church. The conversation went like this:

The first brother said, "You do, of course, agree that Christ did institute a church."

I replied, "If I understand what I think you mean then the answer is absolutely NO!"

The dear brother was shocked and did not know what to say. I urged him to tell me exactly what he meant by the word 'church' and the word 'institute.' He was reluctant to give any kind of clear definition to either word, and kept saying, "But surely you believe Christ established a church." I could not get him to define the terms he was using. I finally said:

"If, by the word *church* you mean a physical organization that was organized and operated exactly like yours, or, put another way, if you mean that Christ established a specific organization that would perpetuate itself and gave that one organization and its leaders the 'duly authorized authority' to be his vicar on earth, then the answer is an emphatic NO—Christ did not 'found, institute, or establish,' that kind of an organized institution with that kind of authority. He did begin to save a people and give those people his Holy Spirit. He also gave apostles to guide them as well as begin the job of evangelizing the world with the gospel. The same apostles were inspired to write epistles that gave those people (and us today) principles and guidelines on how to get along with each other as they served their one Lord. However, he did not 'institute' a physical organization and 'endow it with authority' to be his vicar on earth. That is pure Romanism regardless of what label you put on it."

Needless to say, the discussion accomplished very little because these men refused to use the Scriptures either to define their terms or prove their basic assumptions. They kept saying: "But all Reformed Baptists believe these things." I kept replying, "No, they do not. I am only one of many Reformed Baptists that do not believe your Roman Catholic view of authority. Let us look at your very first question in the light of some specific texts of Scripture."

These brethren would not try to prove their own position from passages of Scripture, nor would they discuss specific texts that clearly contradicted some of their basic concepts. One of the men had a book by John Owen and he kept insisting on quoting from it as if it were the Bible. When I would ask him to show me the specific Scripture texts from which Owen drew his 'facts,' he would go back to the 'all Reformed Baptists believe this' routine. On several occasions when a proof text was given, I would say, "Where does that verse say what your book is saying?" It was like getting a Presbyterian to discuss the 'proof texts' in the Westminster Confession that 'prove' infant baptism.

These men were dear brethren in the Lord, but they had accepted a view of church authority based entirely upon the two basic and wrong assumptions mentioned earlier. They had never examined their basic presuppositions in the light of the Word of God. The Reformed Baptist position set forth in sermons by a few well-known and influential Reformed Baptists preachers were accepted the same way a Roman Catholic accepts the statements of the Pope. It is tragic but true. I should add that two of those same brethren are now openly attacking and refuting the very thing that they were trying to convince me of that day.

I want to set forth my own basic presuppositions clearly so the reader will not only know exactly where I am going, but he will also be able to judge the arguments and see if I am truly establishing the basic facts that are the foundation of my position. Men of a certain temperament will scream "sophistry" and refuse to discuss differences when they cannot defend their position with Scripture. We should be both careful and specific when we set forth the basic presuppositions of our position when discussing differences. It is not enough to reject a given view if we do not put something in its place. Knowing for sure that my view is wrong in no way proves that your view is right. We are not only interested in what the Bible does **not** teach but also what it **does** teach about '*the ekklesia*.'

MY BASIC PRESUPPOSITION

My college philosophy teacher once said, "A philosopher is a blind man in a dark room, looking for a black cat that is not there." In our present discussion, I believe 'the black cat that isn't there' in the Scripture is the clear role model of the physical organization that men call the true New Testament Church when referring to a local assembly (their own) of believers. There just is no such animal in the New Testament Scriptures. I totally reject the two basic assumptions mentioned earlier. The institutionalist is wholeheartedly convinced that he has found the cat that is not there.

I have added a little to my philosophy teacher's bit of wisdom. I have found that the most narrow-minded separatists are the people who sincerely believe that they have actually caught the cat that is not there. They really believe that their particular church is in all points like the one 'true NT role model church established by Christ' and found in the New Testament Scriptures! These people usually accuse all who disagree with them of rejecting the authority of the Word of God and following 'pragmatism and expediency.' Sometimes we rebels are granted the license of pure ignorance or stupidity. However, the usual charge is deliberate unbelief in 'God's clearly revealed truth.'

The 'true NT church' mind-set will always bear the same fruit. There will be a near total emphasis on the local church as an organization and a neglect of the Christian community as a whole. The consuming passion will be to have the right kind of officers exercising total authority and control. There will always be a wide gap between the leaders (usually called elders) and the ordinary Christians (usually called lay persons), and only the 'duly authorized officers' are capable of doing anything spiritual. Wherever these things take a hold, a church will move toward a Roman Catholic concept of authority.

As previously stated, it is no accident that Rome hates the doctrine of the invisible church. One of the essential marks of the true church, according to Rome, is visibility. You cannot exercise control over a spiritual entity, but you can totally control a physical organization. Whenever there is a strong emphasis on the church as an organization instead of an organism, you will invariably find an authority structure that puts all of the power in the hands of the spiritual elite. You may not find the leaders being called "Father," but they will be treated as such. You will find a Roman mentality of church authority when the spirituality of the body of Christ is not emphasized. It will not be long before such a church will consider itself to be the only 'true witness' to the Reformed faith, or Dispensational truth, or Baptist practice, or to whatever particular emphasis created that particular congregation.

The real problem is not separating the so-called 'universal' church from the so-called 'local' church. That particular argument is really only an outgrowth of another and more serious difference. The real error is thinking of the church only in purely institutional terms instead of seeing it as redeemed people who are all bound together in Christ whether they act like it or not. The church surely has clearly defined institutional functions and responsibilities, but that is not the primary emphasis in the New Testament Scriptures.

Every duty enjoined on a believer in the New Testament Scriptures is always based on the fact that he is joined to Christ and therefore joined to every other believer. No one is urged to right behavior toward another believer because they both joined the same local church. The exhortation is always because both are members of the body of Christ, and there is only one body of Christ.

"Hereby we know we love God because we love the brethren" cannot be turned into "because we love the Baptists" or "because we love the particular Christians in our local church." "Exhort one another" is a duty toward all of God's people who profess Christ, not just toward the people who are members of a local congregation.

The real danger in institutionalizing the church is the view of authority that must inevitably follow. Instead of being a 'means of grace' the church soon becomes the 'agent of grace.' The next step makes the 'ordained clergy' to be the only people 'duly authorized' to dispense that grace. It is impossible for such a view to keep the church, especially its leaders, from becoming essential intermediaries between God and the souls of men and women. The evils so clearly and forcefully condemned in the book *Shepherding God's Flock* are a direct result of this institutional view of the church.

HISTORICAL EXAMPLES OF INSTITUTIONALISM

In the next chapter, I will give two examples from history of what I am talking about. I will give a lengthy quote from James Henley Thornwell, a well-known and influential Presbyterian, and also a quote from Hezekiah Harvey, a well-known and influential Baptist writer. Both of these men were totally committed to the assumptions and the mind-set that I reject.

Let me give you the gist of what both of these men say and in the next chapter we will give extensive quotations to show we have not taken them out of context. Here is Thornwell's basic thesis:

> There are amongst us those who hold that God gave us our church-**government**, as truly as He gave us our **doctrines**; and that we have no more right to add to the **church-government**,

which is **Divine**, than to add to the **doctrine**, which is **Divine**[17] (emphasis mine).

Thornwell sets the whole issue in clear focus. The Word of God is just as clear about church government as it is about the doctrine of salvation. We should hold to the system of Presbyterianism just as strongly as we hold to the doctrine of justification by faith simply because the Word of God is equally clear on both subjects. To refuse to do so is to deny the sufficiency of Scripture.

Harvey, the Baptist, does the same thing. The title heading in the introduction of Harvey's book on church polity says it all: "INTRODUCTION: The External Institutions of Christianity **Divinely Instituted**." By 'external institutions,' Harvey means the whole of church polity. He is not talking about baptism and the Lord's Supper. He means exactly the same thing that Thornwell means. He is not just talking about the ordinances, but about the totality of church order and practice. By 'divinely instituted' Harvey means that the church polity he is about to set forth is to be received the same as you receive Scripture itself. Harvey's church polity is as divinely inspired as the message that 'Jesus saves.' The emphasis in the following quotation is mine.

> In the following discussion it is **assumed** [remember the two basic assumptions] that the outward institutions of the Christian religion are of God, and that, **therefore** their **form and order,** as delineated in the New Testament, are of **divine obligation.** The Bible presents a **definite and final**

---

[17] James Henley Thornwell, *The Collected Writings of James Henley Thornwell,* Vol. 4 (Forgotten Books, 2012, originally published 1873) 218.

constitution of the church, the ordinances, and the ministry, and is on these subjects the sufficient guide and the only authority; no man may set aside, alter, or supplement the divine model there given.

… Explicit directions are given respecting the membership, officers, and the discipline of the churches, and the ordinances to be administered…[18]

Harvey and Thornwell are in agreement concerning the truth of the two assumptions previously noted. In their minds, it is the worst of heresy to believe that there is no true New Testament role model institutional church in the NTS. Both of these men are convinced they have caught the cat that is not there. They differ only on the color of the cat.

Both of these godly men ministered in the mid-1800s when both the Southern Presbyterians and the Baptists were struggling with the identical issues that many churches, especially Reformed Baptists, are discussing today. In no sense am I suggesting that either Thornwell or Harvey were not godly Christians or that the Presbyterian and Baptist churches are not great churches. Nor am I saying, "Away with all forms of organization." We must have church structure and some form of institutional organization. I wholeheartedly believe in pastors and elders as well as a clearly defined church order and procedure. I recently left the pastorate of a congregation that elected, under my leadership, three godly elders. However, we never claimed textual evidence for the manner in which we elected them, how long they should serve, and specifically what all of their duties were.

---

[18] Hezekiah Harvey, *The Church, Its Polity and Ordinances* (Rochester, NY, Backus Book Publishers, 1982 reprint) 13, 14.

I agree it is nearly always a good practice that no one should go to the mission field who has not first proven his gifts and calling within the context of a local church. However, I cannot say, "That is the way they did this in the apostolic age." I also agree that the missionary should definitely be under the moral and doctrinal authority of the church, or churches, that support him. In the same breath I must insist that was not true in the apostolic churches. The normal and I think best way today is for a local group of believers to recognize an individual's gifts and calling. It is good if that person can be sent out, be supported, and be under the love and direct discipline of a local congregation. However, I again insist this was not found in the book of Acts.

If God leads someone to serve him under an interdenominational mission board (and despite what the Baptist paper just quoted believes, God has indeed called thousands of Christians to do that very thing), then that missionary should be under the operational and functional control of the particular mission board under which he is serving. We are assuming that the person has complete liberty to teach the truth as he understands it. Can I prove any of this from the Bible? No, I cannot. The reason is that we do not have a single instance in the Bible of **either** a local church or a mission board sending out a missionary. Acts 13:1-4 is often grossly misread in an attempt to prove this. Everything in the apostolic age was directly under the personal control of the apostles. The apostles were 'free-lance' popes responsible to Christ alone. As mentioned earlier, we today are not apostles and therefore dare not act as free lancers under no human control.

Such a working relationship between the local church and an interdenominational mission board in no way contradicts any Scripture. It does violate the basic principle of the 'true church' institutionalist that we are challenging in this book. I am talking about a mindset that **must**, because of its absolutist nature, find in the Scripture what is simply not there, namely, a full blown detailed church order and practice that covers all of church life and each individual work of God's kingdom. The institutionalist must do this in order to be consistent with himself and his false assumptions. He must ultimately come to the conclusion, "There is only one true church model in the New Testament Scriptures and the rest are wrong. Ours alone is the only correct one."

All I am pleading for is that we acknowledge that the NTS are not clear on church government. Let's admit that every system, including our own, is made up of much logic and some Bible texts. Once we admit that, we can then live comfortably with what we believe to be the best system and not accuse those who disagree with our system of either ignorance or rebellion. The institutionalist simply cannot make this admission without giving up his basic assumption or presupposition. We can be wholeheartedly tolerant only when we admit that there really is no cat to be caught. Until we can admit this, we must view tolerance as compromise with truth. It is impossible for an institutional absolutist not to become a consistent sectarian since he is really convinced that he alone has the truth concerning the NT church.

A dear Baptist pastor recently stated in a public meeting that neither he nor the congregation he pastored could support his own daughter and her husband on the mission field. The mission board under which they serve Christ is not totally baptistic nor is it under the authority of a local church. I told the man that I sincerely loved him and respected his right to hold his views. I also told him that I admired his consistency in maintaining his principles in exactly the same manner that I admire the **consistency** of the Puritans for killing the Anabaptists, and others, with a sword. Given their basic presuppositions of theonomic Covenant Theology, the Puritans had no choice but to kill anyone who rejected the authority of the state church. Given the basic presuppositions of this fellow pastor's 'consistent' Baptist theology, he has no choice but to refuse to support his own daughter in a nondenominational mission society because they were rejecting the 'God-ordained authority' of the local church. If situations like this do not make a person look at his basic presupposition and say, "Something has to be wrong some place," then nothing ever will. When men like the Puritans can kill other believers and think they are doing God a favor, discussing anything but basic presuppositions is a waste of time.

THE ROOT OF THE PROBLEM

We must face and deal with two realities today that were both impossibilities in the apostolic age. We did not create the problems nor do we like the confusion created by the problems, but facts are facts and reality is reality. The institutionalist is simply unwilling to face reality. For him to admit to the fact of these present problems is to totally deny the basic presuppositions of his whole approach to Scripture. Here are two things you and I must face and wrestle with that no New Testament believer ever faced.

ONE. It is impossible to conceive that a person in the apostolic age could be a true believer in Christ and not also be a living part of the *ekklesia* of Christ in his area. There is no way you can think in terms of 'Christians' and the '*ekklesia* at Ephesus' as not one and the same thing in their entirety. The believers themselves were the church itself and there was only one church—you did not join it, but rather, you were 'joined to it' by the Holy Spirit. In the apostolic age no one ever got converted in an 'interdenominational evangelistic campaign' and then decided which brand of church he wanted to join. Such a scenario would have been impossible. Just the opposite is true today in many cases.

A strong Baptist once said to me, "Show me one instance in the NTS where a person joined a local church before he was baptized as a believer." I replied, "You show me one instance in the NTS where someone joined a local church **after** he was baptized as a believer." I told the man that his question was a nonsense question and the answer would prove absolutely nothing since he was using a 'joining the church' concept that is not found in the NTS. Believers did not 'join' the church; they were in the church the moment they were born of God! Christ's church existed before any institution was organized.

I am in no way suggesting that it is wrong to 'join a church' today. I believe that whenever possible every believer should be a faithful member of a local congregation in his or her area. He should choose a church where the gospel is preached in purity and support it with his presence and money. I do not say this because believers in the book of Acts joined a local church and therefore it is a biblical practice. Believers did not, at least in the sense we use the phrase 'joining a church,' join anything. They did not have to join what they were automatically a part of by conversion to Christ. The events of church history have changed that situation. Instead of having '**the** _ekklesia_ of (Any Town),' our little village has many different kinds of _ekklesias_. That situation would have been impossible in the apostolic age.

I urge every Christian to join a local church because the Scriptures command Christians to do certain things that can only be performed in our present society by officially becoming part of a particular congregation. However, those things can be performed by joining any one of four or five different denominations. I recommend choosing a church to join based on its own merits and not on the basis of its denominational connections, since there is no one true church organization today. In some towns I would join the Presbyterian church and in other towns I would join the Baptist church, and in still others I might join the Evangelical Free church, or Brethren Assembly, or an Independent Bible church. Likewise, any one of these in another town might be the last church I would even consider.

Again, the true institutionalist must deny that such choices are possible since Christ founded only one church (order). Christ establishing his 'church' and establishing a particular church 'order and government' is one and the same thing to a true institutionalist. His basic problem is that he has confused Christ's _ekklesia_ with an institutional organization.

TWO: It is also impossible to conceive that any believer in the apostolic age had either the option or the problem of choosing between two or more kinds of churches that he could join. Granted, the denominationalism of today forces us to think and act that way, but it must also be admitted that denominationalism in any form is totally inconceivable in the New Testament Scriptures. Whether we like it or not, we must accept denominationalism as a fact of life, but we must also remember that no apostle of Christ would have ever tolerated for a moment the idea of even two kinds of Christians let alone a hundred different kinds! In other words, we are literally forced to cope with a reality that the NTS make clear could never have existed or been tolerated under apostolic authority and control. The institutional legalist simply cannot face this reality. It destroys his whole philosophy of the church.

Can you conceive of the apostle Paul accepting the fact that there were sixteen different kinds of Christian assemblies at Ephesus with each one having a different doctrinal statement and different forms of baptism? That situation is forced on us today, and we must cope with it, but it would have been impossible for such a thing to exist in the apostolic age. It would have been considered heresy of the worst kind.

As we shall see, we must deal with the reality of two thousand years of church history as well as the information in the New Testament Scriptures. We cannot ignore or deny either the facts of Scripture or the events of two thousand years of church history. When we face these two things honestly, we soon discover that the New Testament Scriptures do not give us chapter and verse for answers to many questions raised by the events in church history simply because those questions could not possibly have been raised in the apostolic age. Again, the consistent institutionalist cannot live with such an admission. He simply must find the one true cat in the Scriptures and then duplicate it in detail today. It just has to be there or his whole approach to the doctrine of the church collapses.

People often ask me what the Bible says my attitude, as a Baptist, should be toward a Presbyterian who is a real believer. I always reply, "The Bible does not answer your question simply because it nowhere conceives that there are such creatures as Presbyterians." After a moment's pause, I add, "or such creatures as Baptists." In the early church, saved people were known as 'brethren' without any additional adjective necessary to describe how they differed from other believers; in fact to use any additional adjective to differentiate you from other 'kinds of Christians' would have brought an apostolic thunderbolt down on your head. Can anyone really believe that a particular congregation of believers in Corinth could have gotten away with calling themselves the 'First Baptist Church of Corinth'? Again, such is not the case today. The different beliefs among true Christians today require a label of identification.

In the apostolic age, all of the believers together constituted the *ekklesia* of Christ. You could not be a believer without being part of the *ekklesia*, and you were not part of the *ekklesia* until you were a believer. Everyone in the so-called universal church was also part of a so-called local church, and there was only one local church in town and it was **the** *ekklesia* of Christ. It was neither a Baptist *ekklesia* nor a Presbyterian *ekklesia*. It was the one and only *ekklesia* of Christ in that location. It was all of the believers in that area.

I repeat, such is not the case today, nor is it possible to make it that way.

The same thing is true as it pertains to the doctrine of baptism. A person in the apostolic age was not even accepted as a true Christian until he publicly confessed his submission to Christ as Lord in baptism (Acts 2:37-41). That same thing is true today in a staunch Moslem country or among orthodox Jews. A Jew may confess to be a secret believer but until he is ready to confess his faith publicly by Christian baptism, most Jewish Christians will not accept the validity of his conversion. That same thing is not true among gentile believers in general. Anybody and his cousin are considered saved with or without baptism, church membership, or a changed life. Likewise, most churches will baptize anyone who is not on the FBI's Ten Most Wanted list. Most Baptists feel that a Presbyterian or Methodist believer will get to heaven, but a really consistent Baptist must believe that 'true church' equals immersed believers.

We simply must admit that we face a situation today that could not have existed in the early church. We not only have 'unbaptized' Christians (sprinkling cannot be considered baptism under any circumstance by a consistent Baptist); we even have whole denominations of 'unbaptized' believers. What is even worse, we have 'unbaptized' preachers of the gospel of grace being blessed by God in seeing people saved under their ministries. Some of us even invite these 'unbaptized' believers to preach at our conferences. How can God so continuously bless the efforts of men who deliberately disobey his clear and explicit commandments to be immersed? A consistent Baptist institutionalist has real problems with the Calvins, Luthers, Whitfields, and the over

50,000 evangelical (dare I put the word in print?) interdenominational missionaries around the world today.

The really consistent institutionalist cannot even make the above mentioned men part of the bride of Christ. Calvin, Luther and Whitfield are said to be 'friends of the Bridegroom' but not part of his bride. The Baptist churches alone (the really 'true' ones) are the bride of Christ. It is all so logical and consistent if you are convinced that you truly have caught the cat that is not there.

The situation that existed in the times of the apostles is not true today nor is it possible to make it become true. I am concerned with a mind-set that has a view of Scripture that must force any sincere person to think and act as if the NT situation is either actually true today or that we can recreate it in an institutional sense. The more earnest such a person is, the more separated and bigoted he will become.

It is impossible for us to recreate the early church situation unless we can produce one world church. As long as there are Calvinists and Arminians, sprinklers and immersionists, Covenant theologians and dispensationalists, and all of the other hundreds of distinctions, we cannot have the same situation that existed in the early church. I am one hundred percent in favor of all believers getting together under one roof in one world church, provided of course, it is a 'true' Reformed Baptist roof that I have designed and built personally. In all seriousness, I doubt this will happen in the next ten or twenty years. The real purpose of this book is to help us cope honestly with the events imposed upon us by church history, and at the same time be honest with the inspired writing that God has given us in his Word. It seems to me that it is impossible for us to do either of these things until we get rid of the mind-set that will not allow us to admit openly that the NTS simply do not give us a clear institutional role model church in all of its details.

The institutionalist simply must force the Bible to say far more than it does in order to hold on to his true NT church concept. The lone ranger individualist refuses to use the clear principles that God actually has given in his Word and does his own thing without any authority over him but his own desire. An honest study of Scripture will not allow either of these two attitudes to exist.

Some mission societies and some theological schools have demonstrated that their approach is honest with both Scripture and the realities created by history. They have an authority structure that prohibits individualism and also safeguards doctrinal and moral purity. The obvious and continued blessing of God on their efforts ought to make us question our own spiritual state if we do not experience the same blessings. If our basic assumptions simply will not allow us to have anything to do with these people (because they are 'free lancers' and out of the will of God because they are not under the authority of a local church), we had better look again at our basic presuppositions in the light of Scripture.

Why do many interdenominational schools and mission societies go for over 150 years without changing directions while every local church in town has gone into liberalism? How many local churches in Chicago have become liberal while Moody Bible Institute continues its same doctrinal position and its staunch evangelicalism? Why are local churches and denominational schools the very first organizations to change directions? The answer lies in their view of leadership, authority, and institutionalism.

In the next chapter we will examine very carefully Thornwell's—the Presbyterian, and Harvey's—the Baptist, defense of their position. They are both convinced that there not only is a cat, they are both positive they have caught the cat that is not there.

Chapter Five
Institution or Sheep?

The primary point I have been trying to make is the absolute necessity of having your basic presuppositions established by texts of Scripture and not theological necessity. God made us rational beings and part of that rationality is the need to be logical and consistent in our beliefs and practice. Because this is true, any sincere person will earnestly try to obey the implications of the things that he believes are the will of God. If the person misunderstands the will of God, his sincerity will not keep him from doing some very cruel things in the name of God and conscience. Your conscience is tied up with your creed. If you love God, you must be consistent with both your conscience and your creed.

I believe John Calvin loved God as much as any converted man that ever lived. That is why he would have been a deliberate hypocrite if he would not have had Servetus burned at the stake. His view of sacralism, the wedding of church and state, dictated it was the good and necessary thing to do. This was not a wicked man going against his conscience and committing a horrible crime. This was a man who loved God and was determined to follow his theology at all costs. Calvin did what he did, in his mind, for the glory of God and the good of his church. Because his theology was wrong, his actions brought disgrace to himself and the church. However, we must see that Calvin really had no choice *once he accepted his view of Covenant Theology sacralism!*

I have witnessed some horrible examples of wicked prejudice and bigotry done by good men all in the name of Christ. Churches have been split, families have been divided, and lives have been destroyed by power-mad men who were determined to establish, by any means necessary, the 'true church of Jesus Christ.' The horror stories always begin with a powerful personality believing they alone have the truth. Their church alone is the true New Testament church, and they, as the leaders of that 'true church' are God's vicars on earth. Let me give you two examples of godly men being very wrong. The first is a great Presbyterian named Thornwell and the second is a great Baptist named Harvey.

The emphasis in the following quotation is mine:

> There are amongst us those who hold that God gave us our church-**government**, as truly as He gave us our **doctrines**; and that we have no more right to add to the **church-government**, which is **Divine**, than to add to the **doctrine**, which is **Divine**.
>
> Others...believe no definite form of church-government is of Divine origin... God gave only general principles, and man is to work out of them the best system he can. Thus, one party amongst us holds that Christ gave us the **materials** and **principles** of church government, and has left us to shape them pretty much as we please. But the other holds that God gave us *a Church*, a Constitution, laws, Presbyteries, Assemblies, Presbyters, and all the functionaries necessary to a **complete organization** of His kingdom upon the earth and to its effective operation; that He has revealed an *order* as well as

a *faith*, and that as our attitude in the one case is to hear and believe, in the other it is to hear and *obey*.[19]

Thornwell sets the whole issue in clear focus. The Word of God is just as clear about church government as it is about the doctrine of salvation. We should hold to the system of Presbyterianism just as strongly as we hold to the doctrine of justification by faith simply because the Word of God is equally clear on both subjects. To refuse to do so is to deny the sufficiency of Scripture.

Apart from the very slight caricature, 'has left us to shape them pretty much as we please,' I would wholeheartedly endorse the second position and reject Thornwell's position. It is one thing to say that you use principles in Scripture to build a system, and quite another to say you can do whatever you like. Likewise, it is one thing to build a system on 'necessary consequences' instead of actual Bible texts and **admit** that logic supplied many of your 'facts,' and quite another thing to build a system with logic and then boast that your entire system is totally biblical. It is one thing to believe you have caught the cat, but it is quite another to bring him out of the dark room of your own prejudices and sit him under the clear light of biblical texts of Scripture. This has not been done yet with any of the many 'true NT' cats including Thornwell's Presbyterian cat.

Several more statements from Thornwell should remove any question as to what I am opposing:

> …the duties of carrying out the great Commission were given to the Church, and should be carried out by the **divinely ordained organizations** of the church, namely its **presbyteries**… [Baptists would say "the local church"]

---

[19] Thornwell, *Collected Writings*, 218.

But have we not always boasted that our Church is adequate as *organized in the Scriptures...?* Have we not gloried in our **polity** as **complete** ...? Is our Church competent or is she not competent to do her work? Is she so organized, and so equipped, and so officered, that she can, in the use of her own courts and her own powers, do what her Master has bidden her to do? If not, then openly acknowledge your beggary, and cast about for the best system you can find! If not, then openly acknowledge your impotence, and pronounce your **Divine institutions** a failure![20]

There is absolutely no question what Thornwell believes. He states it clearly. The Presbyterian system of government is just as 'divinely ordained' of God as is the gospel that Jesus saves. Jesus Christ established and ordained the Presbyterian Church, and the Scriptures clearly set forth the whole organization in all of its essential details. The Presbyterian system alone is THE 'true New Testament Church' that Christ established.

Thornwell is a master of argumentation and seeks, like all religious leaders with his mindset, to force you into one of two choices. The implication is that if you can prove one position is wrong, then the other position has been proven to be true. This is very illogical but is used constantly as a method of proving something to be true.

(1) Either sincerely believe and practice the total Presbyterian [or Baptistic if it is a Baptist writer] system because it is the institution given by God in Scripture, or else

---

[20] Ibid., 221.

(2) Admit that you really do not believe that the Bible is sufficient and complete enough for us to do God's work today.

Once you accept the first assumption presented by Thornwell above, then logically you are forced into one or the other of Thornwell's two choices. And who in his right mind is going to choose the second? There is a **third** choice. However, this third choice (which I hold) is not open to the man who accepts the first assumption that the Scriptures give us a divinely ordained role model for the church as an institution. That man is already locked into a position that totally stands or falls on finding the black cat.

I reject both of Thornwell's options as well as his basic assumption. I also reject Thornwell's appeal to equate faith in his system of government with faith in God's clear promises. I can believe in the total inspiration of the Bible as the complete Word of God without believing that it gives me a clear and detailed 'church order.'

> My faith in the adaptation of our **system** is founded on my faith in its **divine origin**. Believing that our Zion is the city of our God [by *our Zion* he means the Presbyterian system] and that he has promised to establish her forever, I am fully persuaded, that, if we would carry out our principles into thorough, practical operation, His presence and spirit would attend us and make our walls salvation and our gates praise.[21] Let us only have faith in the success and efficacy of **Divine institutions**…What we want is faith—faith in the Divine promises, faith in the **Divine appointments**; …[22]

---

[21] You will immediately see how logically the second assumption must follow once the first one is stated.

[22] Ibid., 215, 216.

Thornwell, as you can see, believes that the entire Presbyterian system is just as clearly revealed in Scripture as are the gospel promises. We should receive his system with the same conviction and assurance that we receive the message "Jesus saves." To reject either is to reject the sufficiency of Scripture. The Presbyterian Church, in its entirety and all of its details, is **the** church that Christ established, and it is this church alone that has Christ's authority on this earth to do his work.

You should note the order of concern and emphasis in this last quote. Correct church order is the guarantee of God's blessing. If we would "carry out our principles," then the "presence and power of the Holy Spirit" would come and revive us. As I mentioned earlier, no matter how much of God's Spirit seems to be with another group and its efforts, it simply cannot be a work of God because it is not being done through the 'duly authorized' structure that God has revealed clearly in his word.

Here is Thornwell's final appeal:

> In conclusion, all we ask is Presbyterianism, simple, pure, unadulterated Presbyterianism—the regular, uniform, healthful action of our noble system. … we can have no reason to expect His assistance when we have trampled His **institutions** [Presbyterian polity] in the dust. When the law goes forth, it must go forth from Zion [remember what Thornwell means by this]; and because we have told her towers, and marked her bulwarks, and considered her palaces, and have been **fully assured** that **she** [the Presbyterian Church] **is the city of the Lord of hosts, the city of our God**, we are resolved neither to rest nor to hold our peace till out of

Zion shall go forth the law and the Word of the Lord from Jerusalem.[23]

Thornwell believes that the Presbyterian system is Zion, the true city of God. When truth goes forth, it will go forth from the one true church that Christ founded. That one true church is Christ's only authorized agent on this earth. When I read things like that, I pray that God will never allow men with that mentality to rule our nation. That is the spirit and conviction that has, and will, shed Baptist blood (and the blood of anyone else) for daring to challenge the 'duly authorized' city of God in any way. That is Roman Catholic institutionalism. That was the battle cry of Rome, of the Reformers, and of the Puritans when they put to death any and all that disagreed with 'God's holy truth' as set forth in their particular creed. Their mind-set forced them to do what they did for the 'glory of God and the good of his Church.' The more sincere they were, then the more vehemently they went after anyone that disagreed with God's revealed truth (their creed). We have men today that would do that very thing if they had the civil authority to do so.

BAPTISTS AGREE WITH PRESBYTERIANS

Lest my Presbyterian brethren think I was picking on them when I quoted Thornwell, let me quote from a book by a famous Baptist writer who was a contemporary of Thornwell's. The publisher's foreword, by a contemporary Reformed Baptist pastor, says:

> Finally, I began to see the utter simplicity and scripturalness of a consistent, historic, Baptist view of the church. I saw that

---

[23] Ibid., 172.

many of my Baptist peers had actually departed from the **biblical** teaching of their forefathers. New Testament evidence and **sound reasoning** led me to see Baptist polity as normative for local churches today. [24]

In reading Harvey's book, I find exactly the same spirit and approach to the Baptist 'denomination' that I find in Thornwell and his concept of Presbyterianism. The 'New Testament **evidence**' mentioned above is often hard to find but the 'sound reasoning' abounds on nearly every page. I really have no difficulty with Harvey, Thornwell, or anyone else producing their logical systems and using them to establish order. I wholeheartedly admit that every congregation needs a clearly defined church order, and all of the members should accept and abide by that order. However, when men claim absolute biblical authority for all of the details of their system and accuse those who disagree as 'questioning the sufficiency' of Scripture, then we see a Roman pope wearing a Presbyterian or Baptist robe. If the above writer had just left the word *scripturalness* out of his introduction, I could practice nearly everything in Harvey's book without a qualm of conscience.

The title heading in the introduction to Harvey's book says it all: "INTRODUCTION: THE EXTERNAL INSTITUTIONS OF CHRISTIANITY DIVINELY INSTITUTED."[25] By *external institutions* Harvey means the whole of church polity. He is not talking about baptism and the Lord's Supper. He means exactly the same thing that Thornwell means. He is not just talking about the

---

[24] Hezekiah Harvey, *The Church, Its Polity and Ordinances* (Rochester, NY, Backus Books, reprint 1982) ii.

[25] Ibid., 13.

ordinances, but about the totality of church order and practice. By *divinely instituted* Harvey means that the church polity he is about to set forth is to be received the same as you receive Scripture itself. The emphasis in the following quotation is mine.

> In the following discussion it is **assumed** [here we go!] that the outward institutions of the Christian religion are of God, and that, **therefore** their **form** and **order,** as delineated in the New Testament, are of **divine obligation.** The Bible presents a **definite** and **final constitution** of the **church,** the **ordinances,** and the **ministry,** and is on these subjects the sufficient guide and the only authority; no man may set aside, alter, or supplement the **divine model** there given.
>
> … **Explicit directions** are given respecting the **membership, officers,** and the **discipline** of the churches, and the **ordinances** to be administered…[26]

You will notice that Harvey assumes as a fact in his opening sentence the first assumption mentioned in the beginning of this article; namely, that there IS a true institutional role model church in the New Testament Scriptures. For Harvey, and anyone with his mindset, the details of a complete role model of operating a local church are just as clear and just as 'divinely inspired' as the doctrine of justification by faith. Once you accept that assumption as true, the whole story has been told.

Harvey then lists and attempts to refute two classes of objectors to his position. At this point he is not arguing with those who disagree with his 'Baptist' position. He is arguing with those who reject the idea that there is a complete institutional church role model in the Scripture. He is doing

---

[26] Ibid., 13, 14.

exactly what Thornwell did. Harvey and Thornwell are in total agreement on this point. Their disagreement is only on the color and shape of the cat they have each caught.

The first objectors to his position that Harvey deals with are those that trust 'The authority of the Fathers.' I know of no one in our circles who holds that view as Harvey sets it forth so we shall skip it.[27] Again as with Thornwell I fall into the second class of the objectors, but not the objectors as caricatured by Harvey.

> The other class [of objectors] insists that there is no **divine-required** form of the Christian **institutions**, this being a matter of expediency, to be determined by men according to the ever-changing conditions and needs of human society…
>
> According to these, **all** the different forms of the church and the **ordinances** are equally valid, provided they are adapted to the age and circumstances in which they exist. **Expediency** is the **only** criterion of validity.[28]

Saying there is no absolute 'divinely required' church order and believing that 'expediency is the **only** criterion' are two different things. Rejecting the idea that there is a **total** institutional church role model in the Scriptures and affirming that '**all** the different forms of the church and ordinances are equally valid' is quite a jump. There are very clear **principles** in the Scriptures that must be used and followed when we seek to establish church polity. However, different situations and cultures may be led by the Holy Spirit to apply some of those principles differently. This is the heart of the argument with the institutionalist. He

---

[27] In actual fact, many Baptists treat creeds and Baptist history the same way that Rome treats the dictums of its popes and church fathers.

[28] Ibid., 15, 16.

simply cannot allow a single exception to his church order any more than he could allow deviations to his doctrinal system. It is one ball of wax. You must either believe the Bible gives a clear, total, detailed institutional role model of the church or else you believe in 'expediency.'

The last two paragraphs of Harvey's introduction, like Thornwell's statements, are a classic example of the inevitable mindset that follows the acceptance of the first wrong basic assumption. I have inserted some comments in brackets. I remind you that Harvey is not talking about a few incidentals but the **whole** of church order and practice in **detail**. His basic presupposition and his attitude are identical to Thornwell's:

> True there is in the Bible no **formulated statement** of the **ecclesiastical constitution** that God has **ordained**, but so also there is no formal scientific statement of a system of Christian **doctrines**; yet, as the later fact does not prove that the Bible contains no system of **divine truth**; so neither does the former, that it has no **ecclesiastical constitution**. Plainly, in revelation as in nature, God has set forth manifold **facts** and **principles** [but they are set forth in **specific texts** of Scripture when given to the church as a rule of faith and practice], and as a means of mental and spiritual development has made it **obligatory** on men, by careful investigation and comparison of these, to **evolve** from them the **system of truth** and the **ecclesiastical constitution** he has **ordained**. And **if, as has been show** [*sic*], the Apostles in **establishing these institutions** [a complete role model organization], acted under the guidance of the infallible Spirit, it **necessarily follows** [human logic is essential in the absence of clear scriptural guidance] that their **example** [which was arrived at by logic and not by actual **textual** examples], when clearly ascertained [and our creed, set forth in this book, has **clearly ascertained** (it has?) it], has all of the

force of a **divine precept** and is as obligatory as **divine law**."[29] (emphasis mine).

You can cut that last statement any way you want to and the bottom line will always be: *disobedience to the divine role model set forth in our creed as it has been set forth in this book is disobedience to God himself.* That is Roman authoritarianism whether uttered by a Baptist, a Presbyterian, or a Roman Catholic. That is a mentality that must be avoided at any cost. It equates our system, our books, and our creeds with the words inspired by the Holy Ghost himself. It makes mini-popes out of church leaders and bigots out of those who follow them.

THE ALTERNATIVE

We reject the notion that there is a 'true, New Testament, institutional role model church.' No one can find such a system anywhere in the New Testament Scriptures! We would argue the same as the Anabaptist argued with the Lutheran when discussing baptism. The Lutheran chided the Anabaptist by saying, "Surely, sir, you believe there was at least one small infant in the Philippian jailer's household." The Anabaptist replied, "No, sir. The youngest person in that household was a sixteen-year-old boy." The Lutheran opened his Bible to chapter 16 of Acts and said, "Where, sir, do you find your sixteen year old boy in these words?" The Anabaptist replied, "In the same verse that you find your infant child!"

I am not obligated to prove that something could not possibly be in the Bible. It is your duty to prove it is clearly there if you claim biblical authority for it. I can say that no

---

[29] Ibid., 19.

single 'institutional' view of the church is biblical and therefore not mandatory, not only because there are so many different views, but also because no one view can be established with specific texts of Scripture. However, in this case I can go further and prove that the basic concept of church that is essential to **any** institutional system is itself contrary to Scripture. That fact alone is enough to convince me that the black cat does not exist. Let us consider the following facts:

(1) An institutional role model church simply cannot be found in Scripture by clear exegesis of texts. It must first be assumed to exist and then discovered by a whole series of logical (?) deductions. One must first make the assumption and then look for the evidence to prove it. This is backwards. The truth should come directly from texts of Scriptures. It takes a pretty thick book to prove any system of church order. You have to have a lot of *therefores*, and *we can assumes*, when you have no texts of Scripture. If the Bible was one-tenth as clear about church polity as the institutionalist claims, his book on church order would be very thin and contain mostly Scripture. He could make his statement and give a text of Scripture to prove it. It is the 'sound reasoning' part that takes up so much space.

(2) We could not have such a true New Testament church today without someone having the same authority as that possessed by the apostles. Some Baptists, especially some Reformed Baptists, have actually come very close to practicing this in their view of eldership but none (that I

know of) have claimed apostleship.[30] One Reformed Baptist preacher has convinced himself, and some immature zealots, that he is the 'modern day Nehemiah' raised up by God to purify the twentieth century church.

(3) We could not have a true New Testament church without having the apostolic gifts of the Spirit in operation since it was these gifts that created and operated the early church. Do we have prophets giving us special messages from God today? I agree that some zealots make this claim, but we all know better.

(4) We could not have a true New Testament church unless all of the true believers in our area were part of it and there were no other kinds of churches around. If Paul wrote a letter to the "Church in Any Town," I verily believe that some deluded souls actually believe the mailman would bring the letter directly to their pastor. They literally believe they are the only 'duly authorized' church in town. Is a Bible-believing Presbyterian church just as duly authorized by God as a Reformed Baptist church? Can we accept them as a 'church' when most of their members have not obeyed Christ in biblical baptism? The moment you say "yes" to either of these questions then you must either admit that there is no clear role model for the institutional church or else God has 'duly authorized' some people to disobey God and practice error.

(5) We could not have a true New Testament church today because the NTS not only do not give us details for such a church, they give us evidence of more than one view

---

[30] This is not true of the charismatic movement. Some of them have extended the view of the present-day operation of the New Testament gifts to include apostles with apostolic ability.

of church polity among the early believers themselves. One of the difficult struggles in both the book of Acts and Paul's epistles is resolving the problems that arose simply because they did not have a uniform polity in the various churches. This was glaringly evident in the Jew/Gentile struggles. The church at Jerusalem, under James, would never have agreed to operate that congregation like the Gentile congregations that Paul established.

(6) We should not even **want** churches like some of those described in the NTS! How would you like to be an elder in the Corinthian church? Who in his right mind would accept a call to pastor the Galatians? This last question assumes that local congregations in the New Testament times followed the modern practice of extending a 'call' to an ordained (?) clergyman to come and 'pastor' them. Is this practice (a) biblical, (b) against Scripture, or (c) legitimate expediency? Are we denying the sufficiency of Scripture when we frankly admit we have no clear biblical proof for such a practice? Just because Paul would never have been willing to accept a call to pastor a church already established by someone else (Romans 15:20), does that make it wrong for me to do it today? If so, then I have sinned in this manner at least five times.

I will never forget the first Baptist ordination service that I attended. The chairman kept saying, "We Baptists go by the Book" as he waved the Bible. However, all he did was wave it. He never opened it. I was waiting for him to read about how the early church 'called an ordination council,' how they interviewed the candidate on 'his (1) conversion, (2) call to the ministry, and (3) his doctrinal statement.' I was really waiting for the verses that justified women being on the ordination council (actually there were more women than men but only the men 'laid on hands'). I guess everyone was familiar with the verses 'in the Book' on that subject so they did not bother to quote them. I really learned a lot about 'Baptists going by the Book' that day.

(7) The Scriptures themselves give us no encouragement even to look for a role-model church with each detail laid out. It gives us principles and exhorts us to apply them in wisdom and love to the existing situation. We are to create a church order that is consistent with biblical principles and which also enables us to serve God in unity and efficiency with other congregations that differ with us in church order but preach the same gospel of grace.

WHAT SAITH THE SCRIPTURES?

These statements need to be developed in separate studies. The most important thing is to get a clear picture of what the New Testament Scriptures mean when they talk about the *ekklesia* of Christ. The place to start is in the Word of God and see what it says. We should assume nothing until we first look at what God himself says about the *ekklesia* of Christ. We need to fully acquaint ourselves with some of the specific terminology that the New Testament Scriptures use when talking about the people of God or the church.

One more comment is in order at this point. The philosopher and his black cat story is another way of saying, "Are you sure you are asking a question or are you merely assuming an answer?" And if you are really asking a question, "Are you sure that you are asking the **right** question?" Preachers and theologians are often like politicians; they raise the particular questions that they themselves want to answer instead of really dealing with the basic questions that should be answered. When someone asks the right question, they side step it and deal with another question that was not asked.

When a strong Baptist says, "Show me one single place in the New Testament Scriptures where a person joined the church without first being baptized," we must see this as an invalid statement simply because it makes an assumption about the New Testament *ekklesia* that is not true. It totally institutionalizes the church or *ekklesia*. It reduces the *ekklesia* of Christ to a physical organization or institution that one 'joins.' Nowhere in Scripture is such a concept found.

Another invalid statement is, "The local church did all of the work of God in the New Testament." That is the same as saying "Only Christians did God's work in the New Testament." The church was all of the Christians, and all of the Christians were the church and there wasn't anyone else or anything else. A situation existed then that does not exist today, nor is it repeatable today as long as there is more than one brand of Christian. Can any rational person really believe that his local church (and sister 'true churches') is the only agency through which God is accomplishing any real kingdom work in the world today?

SOME CONCLUSIONS

The implications of this part of this book need to be developed further. My primary concern at this juncture is to prove only one point, namely, that it is impossible for two sincere and honest people to work together if one of them accepts the basic assumptions noted at the beginning of this book while the other does not. It would be like two men being handcuffed to each other and constantly trying to go in two different directions at the same time. All they would do is argue about the direction in which they should go, and they would go nowhere. Nothing but perpetual frustration would result.

It is not a question of brotherly love or tolerance. It is men sincerely holding totally different basic presuppositions. If both men are honest, then it is impossible for them not to try to be totally consistent with the logical implications of their respective views. What an institutionalist would give his right arm to see established I would give my left arm to prevent and *vice versa*. Some men are literally forced to reject fellowship with all that do not 'follow God's truth' as they themselves understand that truth. There are no gray areas with this type of mentality. Everything is either black or white, or else the Bible 'is not a sufficient rule of faith and practice.' Thornwell and Harvey are quite clear as classic examples of this thinking.

These men may sincerely love the Lord but it is hopeless to attempt to work with them unless you put on their straitjacket. The straitjacket is usually a specific confession of faith but it may also be submission to one man's personal authority. These people will always be a thorn in your flesh even as you would be a constant thorn in their flesh. I could no more work with an institutionalist than I could mix oil and water, and it would be just as impossible for an institutionalist to work with me.

I am convinced that the real bottom line is (to quote my late brother Donald) an attitude that says, "Lord, those people are good enough for You, but they are not good enough for us. You made them your sheep and took them into Your sheepfold, but we cannot accept them as obedient sheep and take them into our congregation. You are willing to be their Shepherd, but we are not willing to do the same until we put our peculiar brand on them." This attitude is impossible to avoid whenever a person accepts the basic assumptions that we are discussing.

The true institutionalist is prepared to suffer fully the consequences of being consistent with his system since he believes God revealed that system just as clearly as he revealed the doctrine of the Trinity. He is compelled to 'bar the door' against any and all who will not bow to his creed or authority. His constant fear is what might happen twenty years from now if he should 'open the door.' I sometimes feel like giving these people a forty-penny spike with a note saying, "Driven into the door at the right spot, this nail is guaranteed to keep out Arminians, Legalists, Antinomians, Inter-Denominationalists, Hyper-Calvinists, and all other undesirables." I would then add this note of caution: "The Attorney General of the Church wishes you to know that the same nail will also shut in the love of Christ and the gospel of free grace to sinners."

It is time to start working out the implications of the basic presuppositions set down in this book. I refuse any longer to waste my time and efforts trying to build a biblical superstructure on a non-biblical foundation. I say, "God bless you" to all who are trying sincerely to find the black cat. Look for him as long as you like, but please don't ask me to help find something that does not exist. While you are looking for the cat that isn't there, I am going after the mice that really are there. The woods are full of mice called lost sinners, and some of them are the elect of God. I have been commissioned to seek and find his lost sheep. I have not been commissioned to be the vicar of Christ and establish his one 'duly authorized true church.'

There are a lot of issues that will never be settled on this side of heaven. However, these issues dare not allow us to deny our fellowship with any of God's true sheep. This biblical principle includes far more than many of us have been willing to admit. There are biblical principles laid out in the New Testament Scriptures that forbid a church or a pastor from refusing to accept a believer into fellowship on the same grounds that Christ our Chief Shepherd accepts sinners as his sheep. How dare we claim to be Christ's true sheepfold and then refuse to accept into that fold the very sheep that Christ shed his blood to redeem?

I do not have the slightest hope of convincing any die-hards to agree with me. These people already have both the whole truth and the duly authorized authority to be its sole representative. They have been more than willing to cause divisions and heartache among the people of God just to prove to themselves, and others, that they are God's duly appointed sheriffs. These defenders of God's true church will view me as a traitor to God's clear truth as well as a rebel against God's 'duly authorized authority.' When I plead for biblical tolerance in secondary areas of truth, the institutionalist will be forced to call it 'expediency' and feel it is a compromise with God's revealed truth. He has no choice if he wants to be consistent with his theology.

What I do have hope of doing is saying out loud what many Christians already feel in their hearts! I believe there are many churches, pastors, and battered sheep that are sick of the evils that have attended the 'we are the true church' mentality. They are ready to reach out, accept, and be accepted by, a much broader spectrum of other believers without denying or jeopardizing our sovereign grace convictions. They are ready to get involved in 'furthering the gospel' (Philip. 1:5) instead of building the one true institutional church on earth.

There are many conscientious Christians in rigid, institutional congregations that are sick of the 'we four/no more' mentality that has destroyed any meaningful fellowship with other believers because 'these people are not really in our camp.' These Christians are tired of seeing the Arminians get all the converts while their own local church efforts consist of witnessing Calvinism and 'true church' doctrine to these 'immature and untaught victims of easy-believism.' I believe I speak to many hearts that long to see sinners saved and changed in their own assembly, instead of wistfully seeing it happen in other places—and bravely trying, in vain, to justify why it is not happening in their own assembly. Is your heart and conscience asking the following question: **"If our church has the most truth and the only true biblical authority, why doesn't God use us to save his true sheep instead of using those people that we are constantly opposing and criticizing?"**

Maybe the answer to that question is far more obvious than many of us have been willing to admit. Maybe the people and churches that have been criticized for not preaching 'the true gospel' have at least faithfully preached the gospel as they understood it. Is it not a fact that these people preach the Lord Jesus Christ himself as the only way to be saved, and do they not also urge sinners to flee to him for salvation? Must we not also admit that many of our 'true New Testament churches' have made the establishing of 'the one true institutional church' to be the primary goal of their preaching and practice? And is it not also tragically true that these same 'true' churches have miserably failed to (1) preach the gospel to the sinners in their own immediate area, or (2) heal and help the wounded sheep under their own care?

I do not attend your church and therefore have neither the right nor the ability to judge it. However, you have both the ability and the responsibility before God to judge whether your church is more interested in the souls of men, or if its primary concern is the 'authority' of the church and its leadership! You are responsible to your Lord to judge if your church exhibits the love of Christ, the fruits of the Spirit, and is genuinely interested in people, or whether your church is primarily interested in church order, the authority of the elders, and criticizing everyone for 'false evangelism' while you have no real evangelistic effort to reach the lost.

Scripture Index

Made in the USA
Las Vegas, NV
12 June 2021